Down the Drain

A Commentary on Society's Shift

By

Vincent Mancino
With Jeff Scott

Down The Drain

A Commentary on Society's Shift

www.downthedrainsociety.com

Writing by: Jeff Scott

ISBN: 1453773800
EAN-13: 9781453773802

Down the Drain

A Commentary on Society's Shift

CONTENTS

FOREWORD
BY
Vincent Mancino

This book is about shifts in our society that I've noticed have created bigger problems and are affecting many different areas of life and our country. Some of the things I talk about in this book are a compilation of grumblings I've heard other people complain about. Some of it makes complete sense and some of it doesn't. Don't shoot the messenger. All I ask is that you think about it. Chew on it for a bit. Though I'm sharing some of my beliefs, I'm not saying that I'm always right. I talk about some of it just to get some debates going in an attempt to get our country back on track. Trust me, I'm smart enough and dumb enough to know that the stuff that flows between my ears isn't always the best or the smartest. I do, however, think that this book is real and authentic. I think we are a society that has forgotten that it's okay to be real and it's okay to be yourself. Everyone doesn't have to agree with me or you, or for that matter, they don't even have to like you.

There's fun to be had in life when you're able to disagree with others, believe in yourself, and like who you are. It's life!

I'll probably say some things that will piss some people off and that's okay, it doesn't really bother me. I hope you, the reader, view this book as providing common sense, being driven, being funny, and even being annoying at times. I think that some of the things I write about are simple and I'm shocked that the whole country doesn't see it the way I do. I'm guessing that everyone needs an excuse; everyone needs a villain or a reason to not look in the mirror. Maybe, just maybe, I can get one parent, one politician, or one person to see things just a little differently. This is my attempt to do my small part, to help us from turning into a society that doesn't believe or rely on itself and doesn't end up getting gobbled up by China or some other country that becomes stronger.

Is anyone seeing what I see? Is there any way to change, to reverse the problems of a country that was at one time considered great by every nation on the planet? Do you remember when people from all walks of life used to want to live here? Now it seems a good majority just want to be here to infiltrate and tear down our country, our lifestyle. If you don't understand what is happening, this erosion to our great democracy, and if you don't find this is very upsetting, then you're probably a part of the *Down the Drain* crowd that I'm concerned about. You might possibly even get pissed off that you paid for this book or someone gave it to you as a hint.

There has been a lot happening to erode this great country of ours through the softening of the young minds that could have grown and continued to sustain our superiority in the world. I don't want to be the guy running around and declaring that the sky is falling or the end of days are near (like in the movie *Red Dawn*), but I'm here to make a very plausible comment: "The sky is falling! Get out your doomsday signs!"

I hope that through this book, I can reinvigorate, at the least, a part of the masses to question what they've done and have accepted as "just the way it is" way of life. If I can get just one person to not blame everyone else for their failures then I've done something good.

When I think about my grandparents' generation, I realize that as they grew older they must have wanted desperately, at some point, to get out, move on, kick the bucket, take the last train home, or just up and die. They began shaking their heads when they saw kids like Elvis and the Beatles become popular. If they were around long enough to see the eighties' glam rock scene then I'm sure their head-shaking stopped and was replaced with a dropped jaw. They now had definitive proof, complete knowledge, that this was the beginning of the end.

Now, I don't believe that the eighties' glam rock scene changed how the world operates, other than teaching guys to stay away from Aquanet and make-up; the erosion I'm talking about came from a much different source.

Many grandparents have wondered what happened; who pulled the rug out from under them. That's the question I want to humorously, yet seriously, answer. Throughout this book, I make commentary on personal observations I've had and I willfully stick my neck out to say…or shout…"What the hell were they thinking!" If you are offended by anything I write about, well, go point your finger at someone else and know that you're who the book was meant for.

Good readings—or possibly, good riddance?

Vincent Mancino

How About a Thank You Card?

The phone begins to ring and my wife nudges me to answer it. Rubbing my eyes, I look across my king-sized bed toward the nightstand where my alarm clock sits with its neon blue digits that read 4:00 a.m.

"Who could be calling at this hour?" I ask myself.

Upon answering, I hear a woman's voice which sounds sultry and very seductive.

Softly she says, "Good morning, Mr. Mancino."

I slowly peek over my shoulder toward my wife, wondering if she can possibly hear what I hear. The woman continues as I follow each syllable and begin to wonder which of my crazy friends is playing a prank.

"Mr. Mancino, I just want to thank you for yesterday and the day before. You've made my world a better place and I wish there were more of you out there."

Once again, I glance over my shoulder as though I've done something terribly wrong and my wife would be standing with a divorce decree and pen in her hand. I feel so guilty and I'm sure I must be dreaming.

The phone line clicks dead and my wife asks who it was. I sit up in wonder, and again, rub my eyes. "I don't know who it was, but they knew me."

From my room, I hear a beep in the kitchen and I know that my automatic coffee maker is beginning to drip a strong, hot cup of joe. I'll need to take a shower, shave, and get dressed for work. I packed my bags last night for my 6:00 a.m. flight. I'll be on the road for a week of corporate meetings.

When I get to the kitchen, I smile as I think about the voice on the phone. That was just weird—nice, but weird. I wonder which prankster friend of mine got some woman to call me at this ungodly hour. It must have been someone who knew I was getting up to leave town. Pouring my cup of coffee I begin downing about enough vitamins to kill a small horse. I take my first sip and inhale the fresh aroma. Standing in front of the kitchen sink, I look out the windows and discover through squinting eyes that there is a crowd of people across the street waving and holding signs, banners with my name. A man thrusts himself to front of the group and kneels with his placard that says, "Thank you for all you do, Vincent." Another sign declares, "Vince, we really appreciate you," and a third sign I can barely make out, but then it comes clear: "Mancino for President!"

I shake my head and consider pinching myself, asking, "What the hell is happening?"

I hear a knock at the front door. Looking at the wall clock, it's now 4:15 a.m. Instead of opening the door, I peek through the peephole and see a guy in a black-and-white suit. He stands there with a smile on his face and I can't help but open the door.

"Can I help you with something?" I ask the man.

"Hello, Mr. Mancino. I have a limo waiting for you. I just got done working and thought that maybe I could give you a lift to the airport. You know, it's not every day I get to do something for someone like you."

I take a deep breath and instead of asking him what all this is for, I tell him I'll be ready in thirty minutes as I still have to apply my hair-care products to hide all the grey I've acquired from helping to hold up the weight of the world. I know I must be dreaming. So, why not take a limo to the airport? I'm sure when I wake up my wife will be pulling the blankets off of me and telling me I'm going to miss my plane.

Everything feels so real. Is this what they call a lucid dream? You know, when your dreams coincide with reality. In the shower, I feel all warm, just like I would in my bed. Getting a little soap in my eyes…of course, that's why I'm rubbing my eyes. It's not that I've just woken, but really, it's just a part of the dream. Wow! It's just incredible how the mind works. After getting out of the shower and dressing, I hang my jacket over my arm and grab my suitcase. I kiss my wife on the cheek as I strut to the front door in anticipation of my limo ride. This is the best dream ever. I grab my briefcase and open the door. The limo guy is still there. Man! When am I going to wake up?

"Let me take that for you, Mr. Mancino." He grabs my cases and smiles.

Just out on the street sits a stretch limousine. "Okay," I say to myself, "I'm getting a ride to the airport." This dream is way too cool to even think about calling out to my wife. If she wakes me now I'm going to be pissed. As the driver opens my door, I hear the people across the street cheering.

"My god, there must be a hundred of them," I mumble.

"Oh yes, if not more. They just wanted to show you a little appreciation for going to work today and paying all the taxes that you do."

I can't get over it. This has never happened before. I'm always made out to be the bad guy because I earn a lot of money. Even the president can't help but to make me look evil as he berates people like me, the 10 percent that pay roughly 70 percent of everything.

Well, it's about time. Okay, honey, you can wake me up. Sweetie? Sweetie? Wake me up or I'll be late.

Sure enough, the buzzer has gone off, and then, so does the alarm.

"Sweetie, you're going to be late for your flight." My wife nudges from her side of our warm bed.

I drag myself out of bed and slightly snicker about the sexy and sultry voice of my dream. In the kitchen I pour my cup of coffee and as I take my first sip, I glance out the windows. Nothing! Crap!

Oh well, I guess if there's going to be any appreciation from people for the amount of dollars I put into the system each year, it's only going to come in a dream. You'd think a guy could at least get a thank-you card. You know, maybe the government can at least show its appreciation by sending me a nice hand-written thank-you card. They know who I am, they cash my checks. Is a freakin' thank-you card too much to ask?

I saunter over to the front door and though at this point I do realize it was only a dream, still, I open the door and look outside. There's no driver, no limo, and no crowd of people to cheer me on. Why do I keep at it? Why do I put myself through the grind? I love my wife and kids and want to give them a great lifestyle, but really, I work my ass off and I'm not being able to find the upside, the incentive to keep going. I could downsize everything and live a less comfortable life, but that's not my personality, my vision of myself. I've never wanted to do things in mediocrity. Play hard, play smart, and win is my strategy. Mediocrity, that's for the minds of the masses.

I find myself continuously asking, "Why do I get up so early for work every day?" "Why am I always portrayed as the bad guy?"

•   •   •

The taxi is here to take me to the airport. As the driver takes my suitcase, I look at him and ask, "You ever thought of driving a limo?" He just looks at me with a blank stare, not sure how to answer the question.

Sitting in the back seat, the street lights we pass are just bright enough give me a clear view of the driver's profile. "Where are you from?" I ask, all the while knowing he's not American. He doesn't seem to hear me as he concentrates on a lane change. I guess it doesn't really matter where he's from, America's a melting pot.

I begin to think about this driver taking me to the airport and I ask him, "How long have you been here in this country?"

"I have been here for five years," he replies.

"What made you move here?"

He looks back toward me for a quick second, smiles, and then, almost boastfully, says, "I love America. Here you have a choice to be anything you want to be."

Thinking about his reply, I ask, "Are you going to school or anything?"

"Oh yes. I have to. I have a wife and two children and I want a great life for them."

"So you go to school and support your family. Does your wife work?"

"Yes, but only at a department store. She too goes to school."

"So who watches the kids?" I for some reason had to know.

"My mother lives with us and watches the children. We are not rich, but we are making ends meet and reaching our goals."

I stay silent for a moment, thinking about this guy. He can't be more than thirty years old and he is doing more than many who've grown up here.

When he pulls over to the airport curb he jumps out to quickly open my door and the trunk where my cases are stored. Taking cash from my pocket I hand him the fare and a tip.

He smiles, "Oh thank you. As they say, cash is king."

"Tell me something," I begin to ask, "Do you pay taxes?"

"Honestly, no one knows what I collect in tips so I don't declare it all."

For some reason, I'm only semi-disappointed. We all need cash, to have some fun with or to meet some of our expenses, but there's got to be a better way to make sure everyone pays their fair share.

•　　•　　•

I tell this little story because I want to make a point: taxes weigh heavy on my mind. I am in a higher tax bracket than the masses and though I enjoy the comforts of life that I've achieved, there's still something in the back of my mind that says, "Vincent, you're being cheated."

So I ask you, shouldn't the guy paying $10K in taxes get a little better treatment than the guy paying $0? Shouldn't the guy paying $100K in taxes get a better deal than the guy paying $50K? I suggest that the higher the taxes you pay the more benefits you're allowed. Perhaps you get a pass for private and faster roads to drive on, shorter lines in the airport, or an exact appointment time for the cable guy. What about faster Internet? Just give them something to let them know they're really appreciated. Give them anything that allows them to make money faster and easier so they can continue to subsidize the whole country.

You could even make it more convenient to pay taxes, but whatever you do, don't make the high taxpayer out to be the villain when in fact they're the good guys.

Everyone that pays $0 in taxes should be made to help out those who do pay. Have them pull weeds, run errands, serve as someone who places wake-up calls. Something! Anything that says—thank you.

There are many obstacles to overcome in this life and many lessons to learn, I've had my share, but it seems that the idea about being cheated isn't something that is easily corrected. It doesn't appear to be in my control. America is in such a terrible financial fiasco that they say our children's children will be paying for this debacle. Yes! Generations to come! Is there truth to this? How will our children's children be able to pay? Are they going to start actually growing money on trees? There has to be a better way!

Though I don't like taxes, I do realize they are a part of life right now. I also think that there are other alternatives to collecting exorbitant amounts from the wealthy every time some new problem arises because some bureaucrat got his panties in a bunch and can't get his state's budget in order.

I would love it if my tax money went for roads, bridges, real education, national security etc... Let me decide where it goes, just stop the wasteful spending. The government needs to stop acting like a college kid who just received his first credit card.

I want to talk for a minute about two taxes that I think would work perfectly. You've heard of them before: the flat tax and the consumer tax. When I'm done explaining my thoughts on these two great solutions, I'll explain why I think the government won't change to either one. You may not agree with my reasoning, but just the same, it's food for thought.

FLAT TAX
No one will ever change my mind to believe that a flat tax doesn't make sense. No matter the gross income a person makes, they should pay 20 percent to live in this country. Think about how much tax revenue we'd gain if just 50 percent of the non–tax-paying public had to contribute instead of getting off for free.

Why should people who make more money have to pay a larger percentage in taxes? If this made sense, then the rich should have to pay more for jeans, more for a cheeseburger, more for toilet paper... Imagine if there were a different price for everything and it was based on your income. If you make more than $50K then you pay $75 for a pair of jeans. If you make less than $50K then your price for those jeans is $50. It seems ridiculous and strange for something to work like this, but that's the exact idea behind our tax structure.

We know that when millions of cars are pumped full of petrol each day that the taxes collected are supposed to keep our roads paved. The residential and rental property taxes collected are supposed to keep city workers busy earning an income and the schools running like a well-oiled machine (except for the actual education part).

The 20 percent flat tax should go to different things like infrastructure, R&D, public safety (fire/police), to make life more sustainable for everyone. We could also have a 5 percent flat tax that goes to the state one really resides in, not just the one they use for an address to avoid taxes.

With this flat tax system, the federal and state governments would have to work on a budget the same way all businesses are expected to. Politicians wouldn't be allowed to raise taxes just because they can't stay within a budget, and also, they wouldn't be allowed to penalize the wealthy for doing well. What about the corporations that create jobs, and yes, donate millions of dollars while sponsoring charities? Penalize them for doing well too? I read a quote the other day in the *New York Times*:

"It's past time for the wealthy individuals and corporations to carry more of the burden."

This makes absolutely no sense to me. Right now, the wealthy individuals and the corporations carry most IF NOT

ALL of the burden AND IT'S STILL NOT ENOUGH? Shouldn't every citizen have the right to keep at least 70 percent of their own money? They earned it. How about this, someone could post a quote that reads:

"The country is now bankrupt because we've soaked the wealthy individuals and corporations dry. You're on your own. Good luck!"

It's a despicable shame that we don't charge people for the public amenities they so freely use. It teaches them nothing, other than that they can keep taking and they don't have to be responsible for their actions or contribute to the pot. If we had the second tax I'm about to discuss, consumer tax, our country might not be in this world of financial hurt. Am I the only one who read the story of the little red hen?

CONSUMER TAX
This too is a great idea. With a consumer tax plus a flat tax, regardless if one gets paid under the table, when they purchase goods they will have to pay their fair share. With this method there is no escape. Some might argue that a poor person might not be able to pay the higher consumer tax. Well, I say there are two ways to handle this: 1. Get out and make more money, or 2. Don't tax food, shelter or clothing, the basics that people truly need.

Food would have a registered category in the stores and junk foods wouldn't fall into this category. Same with clothing; there are certain stores that people without a lot of money will go to and do their shopping. These stores can have un-taxed clothing. The higher-end stores would have tax because they don't offer an exact necessity for living. I kind of laugh about the consumer tax because it'd be the first time our country isn't so hell-bent on getting rid of the illegal aliens. Let me add here, though I don't agree with illegal immigration, they really do spend a lot of money here, collectively. It's unfortunate that we haven't figured out how to collect when they use medical services and other public amenities.

The consumer tax doesn't have to be high. It could be at the current 6–9 percent levels or 1–2 percent higher. This way, since no one is exempt, believe it or not, there would soon be a surplus.

There is an argument that says the stores now become our tax collector. So what! They're already a tax collector as it presently stands. The cash registers can be changed to read whatever is desired. We've already seen that every time a governor can't meet his state's budget they add a tax and re-rig the register to collect such and such amount. They've done it with cigarettes and soda bottles…the bar codes are set to agree with the register on the amount to charge for whatever the product.

Tell you what; to make things fair, for the stores that have to change their registers and input fresh information, the government would pay them for their time and effort. This could entice the stores to be even more of the collector they already are.

Years ago, I read a study about a group that proved a consumer tax just on tourism alone would pay for all of our military defense system. Of course, after 9/11, tourism was down and our defense budget, because of the wars in the Middle East, became beyond exorbitant.

Either one of those two taxes would help to set our country straight. Oh, and while we're at it, we should probably require our politicians to attend night school to take economics courses—on their dime. Hopefully, if they didn't nod their way through class, the way they do their terms in office, they'd learn that you're not supposed to spend more than you make—on a personal level as well as government.

While we're at it, sending our politicians to night school, we should be requiring all citizens in this country to take a course in economics. Everyone should be forced to take a literacy as well as comprehension class. Politicians will always win the vote when they preach about creating a much better life for the poor by taking from the rich. Many people want the best in life, but they don't want to earn it.

The course in economics doesn't have to be difficult, but more so, something that teaches people to be in control of their finances and that they too should contribute to the welfare of the country, not just the welfare of their pockets.

Hey, here's a crazy idea. It could seem a bit reckless, and I know any politician reading it would choke, laugh, or spit up blood, but I'm going to throw it out there anyway: for every $100k someone spends in income tax, they get one year off of paying taxes. Can you imagine that? An actual incentive to pay a tax! There could be rewards for people that pay lesser amounts, but are still contributing. Imagine how much money could be pumped into the US economy in that year off of paying taxes. Some people would actually want to pay taxes to get the year off instead of avoiding taxes like they do now.

Wouldn't it be nice to get a little thank you for paying all the taxes: "Here, you can have a year off. Go on, save a little more for you and your family. Go buy that sports car you always wanted, it'll help put an auto worker back in the plant."

We've got to do something, folks, because right now we're paddling up a fast-moving river and it doesn't look good.

•   •   •

Anyone can get mad at me for suggesting that I expect the average everyday citizen to take a class in economics, but really, would it be so bad? What would that teach the little children, who may eventually end up on the welfare system because they learned by example, what they saw their parent/s do?

Basically, I'm trying to prevent the failure of our country. There isn't enough emphasis on finance with the younger generation. Sure, they learn some things in school about money, but how much do they learn about taxes?

Let me tell you how much, NONE! Why? Because our tax system is so screwed up, things change so rapidly, that by the time a teacher could understand the tax rules the information would be outdated, not applicable to the day.

Of course, I'm ranting and raving about this and it may seem a bit foolish to think that we can change, but then again, show me where we have ever changed for the better when it comes to taxes and creating a better system that truly flows on a fair basis.

My take on this, the part that bothers me the most about the tax structure, is that not only do the "wealthy" pay the majority of the taxes, as previously mentioned— stats of 10 percent of society paying 70 percent of the taxes collected—but the part that drives me most crazy…is watching a politician speak and condemn the wealthy. They sure don't have a problem taking more and more dollars from them. Why do thieves rob banks? That's where the money is. Why do the politicians tax the wealthy? That's where the money is. There is one great difference between the thief and the politician: the thief doesn't point a finger at the bank and declare it to be evil or wrong for having so much money. Everyone should have to lease time in the United States. Everyone should have to pay taxes!

•   •   •

Our government is telling the higher-income wage-earners to pay 35–45 percent taxes. They focus on this group with laser-like precision and it cracks me up because I'm shaking my head and asking, "Why aren't they going after the 40 percent of Americans that don't pay anything in taxes?" On a side note: How the hell do people who pay nothing in taxes get a refund check? Isn't that welfare?

As an example: Out of 300 million people in this country, you could take a majority of them, 200 million, and ask them to contribute just $100 per month for the next twelve months (not impossible). In the first month there would be 20 billion dollars. In the course of a year, there would be 240 billion dollars. Then after the politicians got done siphoning off their cut, we'd have at least 15 million to throw towards our trillions of dollars of debt. Of course, I'm kidding about the politicians siphoning off that much, they only think they have deep pockets, because they somehow manage to forget it's OPHEM (other people's hard-earned money).

It's unfortunate and a disservice to the average Joe to not hold him accountable for supporting this great nation. The fact that the government won't even consider asking the majority of low or medium wage-earners to contribute, is a sign that they don't know anything about balance.

By the way, for those reading this that are of medium-to-low–wage incomes, getting a tax return isn't a contribution. You've let the government use your money free of charge, and you don't get it all back. When I pay, I won't see a dime in return…my contribution takes care of you. That's giving, and that's what paying a tax does…it takes care of others. Please get out and contribute.

•　　•　　•

I said I'd discuss why I think the government won't change to a flat tax or consumer tax. The reason: CONTROL! If you've ever seen the Internal Revenue Service's book concerning tax laws and rules, you'd notice it's so thick that to get through it with any real understanding of what the law is would be an incredible feat in itself. It's like hiding a written sentence in a 500,000-page document and telling someone that if they can find the written sentence in ten minutes, they win. The government and the politicians don't want you to win. If you do, they lose control.

The tax system is a volunteer system, yet everyone can be punished by imprisonment if they don't volunteer. Let's change the way our system works and let's do it now. There are hundreds if not thousands of people in jail for "tax evasion." We make them out to be bad guys and I get the fact that they broke the "volunteer rules" but at least most of them were putting money into the system. They aren't sending it to a foreign land to buy property such as some illegal aliens do. We're all leasing some kind of time here in the US, and a consumer tax would make everyone pay their fair share.

If I defined the word volunteer, which doesn't mean "agreed to by force," you would know that the IRS and the government are in cahoots. They want to remain in control at the peril of our country's greatness. Let's change this to a new tax system, one that is truly fair for all. To use a metaphor: there is nothing wrong with taxes that create a strong and supporting roof over our head, but we need to build a better roof that protects us all evenly.

We are a smart nation, and we can come together as a team like never before. People like me everywhere across this country are feeling cheated. Look at the Tea Party groups that are sprouting up everywhere. People are truly sick and tired of the current system. Oftentimes, they're made out to be rebels or just a bunch of lunatics when they join these groups and picket on the streets for everyone to see. News stations are trying to label them as wacko, but in all sincerity, they're just like you and me, they want a better system that creates an equal contribution from everyone.

Write to your congressman and send them the local night-school listing for an economics class. Then, if you're feeling rather generous, someone please, send me a freakin' hand-written thank you note.

Who Brings Twinkies
To The Game?

It's 8:30 on a Saturday morning and I'm surrounded by two types of kids. Some are excited to be up and out for an early-morning soccer game and others are ready to go back home to their bed. The attention span of six-year-olds on a weekend morning is usually kept secure by a bowl of cereal and the latest cartoon, but that's in the comfort of one's home, not here on the soccer field.

As the ball gets kicked between players, I find myself being caught up in the action. I'm having a ball coaching the kids—no pun intended—and though I want the kids to have fun and learn about the game, winning wouldn't be so bad either. Is that a crime? Is the desire to win wrong? In this day in age, it appears to be.

I hear a parent yell out to her kid, "Oh Stevie, we're just here for the fun. No one wins or loses. It's just a game for fun. You're doing great, honey!" Keep in mind that this parent hasn't watched a minute of the game and has been chatting, texting, and anything else other than caring about the game. Stevie doesn't know if we are playing soccer, hockey, or chess for that matter and doesn't seem to think listening is a big deal either.

Okay, hearing this mentality, when it comes to sports, just drives me crazy. I understand the admonishment of getting your kid to believe in themselves, telling them that they're great, but when the kid is rolling around on the grass like he's on fire, please, please, please understand that sports are a competition of skill to be won, and through this venue, your child has a great opportunity to learn how to be agile and focused.

Outside of professional sports, competing is a lost art. It's a huge deal in the lessons of life. Winning isn't a big deal, but wanting to win and trying to win is, and it means everything in respect to the growth and maturing of our kids. We've forgotten how to give a real effort in this country. Our kids need to be taught how to compete correctly and not let them off the hook because things aren't going their way. Just showing up doesn't create greatness.

Finally, taking a break as halftime rolls around, it's now 9:15 and I've got the kids on the sideline discussing what we need to work on while in the game. Coaching a bunch of goofballs is something I enjoy and if I can do anything to make a kid into a better player, I'll be direct and point out what they need to work on to better develop their skills.

Just as I'm rooting the kids on, letting them know that they are doing great and could step up their game just a tad, one of the parents in charge of the halftime snack begins handing out Twinkies and some sort of chocolate drink. I look at my watch. "Twinkies and chocolate?" I say to myself. "This parent is handing out Twinkies and some sort of chocolate drink at 9:15 in the morning?"

My brain wants to bark out, "What the hell is wrong with this picture!" but I bite my tongue. Why couldn't she have brought quartered oranges and water?

I realize not everyone eats healthy all day, every day, but come on! Then I think about it for a moment. Of course, this is why America is in the shape it is. Twinkies right in the middle of a game!

Now, I'm not totally opposed to junk food, I think it's fine in moderation, but again, 9:15 in the morning? That's almost right up there with crackin' a beer at 7:00 a.m. before heading to the gym on a Tuesday before work.

·   ·   ·

You know how they say that forty is the new thirty? Well, I believe that last place has now become the new first place. I played sports throughout my childhood and I don't once recall getting half the things kids get today. The most amazing thing to me is that everyone is rewarded no matter the outcome, win or lose. Seriously? A trophy for everyone? Who thought this up and why? I dare to say that whoever the culprit is that designed and awarded the same size of trophies for first, second, and third place on down, regardless of the level of play, probably never earned or put in the real work necessary to receive a bigger trophy than the next guy.

When did we forget that playing a sport is about competing and that the winners are supposed to get the bigger reward? It's about bringing your best ability to the arena and showing the other team your skills. Next thing you know, we'll stop giving grades out in school. Everyone will get an A+ just for showing up. All C students will be allowed into Yale, because it's only fair. Should we cancel the Olympics?

Some of the best games I ever played while growing up were against guys that I knew were better than me. It made me step up and try my absolute best to prove I was great, or at the least, that I could provide a tremendous challenge to their skill level.

Why isn't this still happening in America? When did we, for the lack of a better word, pussify sports? Go Google this word, pussify. I think it was made up by the great comedian George Carlin. You'll see that it defined as: The state in which a society becomes less and less tough. That sounds about right, doesn't it?

Who made the decision that it's okay to lose? I've got kids and let me tell you...they keep score on everything and so do all of their friends. If you don't think that kids care about winning then take them fishing and you'll have proof. The kids will count every fish they catch versus the number another kid caught. You might even hear a kid respond with something like, "You might have caught more, but mine are bigger."

Life is a competition. Even the TV show *The Biggest Loser* is about the biggest winner. I teach my kids how to be a good winner and a good loser.

When I was a kid, if you weren't good, you sat on the bench. Now, in today's game, a kid can't sit out more than two innings, a quarter, or whatever the rule says. I don't mind this rule as long as the kid pays attention and tries his best. I can't stand the rules where everyone gets to play but not even try. A person can even be terrible at sports...

that's alright…just try. I do believe that everyone should get a chance, so please just give it your absolute best!

What's the message to the players who want to win, but they also know little Johnny is going to pay more attention to the daisies in right field than watching for the ball coming his way? I guess it could be construed as a lesson to the serious players that throughout life, one will have to deal with those who don't care about results, about winning.

A little losing should hurt and kids should care about getting better and winning. What's so hard about going home after a game, going outside, and actually practicing while the information is fresh in one's head?

I was coaching during one particular football season and I had this kid on the team that was a good player when he got the ball, but when he didn't get it, he didn't try much. I might mention that he was missing in action a lot.

One day, I get a notice that he's been sick with the flu all weekend. I figure this is warning that the kid won't be available for the game. Well, not only does he show up for the game, but while his parents are watching him from the grandstands, he walks out to the huddle while I'm talking and in his hand is junk food, which he is heavily munching on. Other kids in the huddle get involved with wanting some of his snack, and instantly, all concentration is lost. Again, what the hell are parents thinking? First off, if your kid has the flu, don't send him in the middle of the mix to get everyone else sick; and secondly, don't just sit idle in a moment when you could be teaching them something of value…like respect. Support and cheer for your team, but don't make them hungry for snacks in the huddle.

•   •   •

We've been sending the wrong message for far too long. If you've ever been in a position of hiring employees, you'd agree when I say that it's easy to recognize the kids who played sports seriously versus the kids who were there for the snack. This is what America has come to. Day after day there are young adults in the working world who have been weaned on the false idea that nobody wins or loses.

I've been around high producing organizations for a long time and have learned a thing or two: finding a good indicator of what one has to work with is important. Ex-athletes whose results are down are often taken aside (like in a huddle) and almost instantly, they find their team spirit and tackle their job with a vengeance. As for the snacker…they give excuse after excuse as to why their performance is down. I've seen and heard it when I first started out in the business world and it still happens today. Yes, some things never change.

I'm leaning toward the belief that in twenty years our country will have zero, nada, none, no high producers in the business world because no one will want to work to be number one. Everyone seems to think they should make all the money with little effort or work and if we keep going on the path we're on, there will be laws prohibiting you from getting rid of them.

So, you might ask why I relate everything back to a winner or loser mentality and sports. It's been said that

90 percent of our personality is made up by the age of six. Somehow, I can believe that. Yet, on the other hand, I think anyone and everyone can change if they want to. I'm not saying a person has to change, just that they can.

Around the age of six is when most kids really start getting introduced to sports. Some might have played in a pre-rookie league at an earlier age, but six is usually a good beginning stage. It also happens to be the age when kids begin hearing the big lie, "no one wins or loses." So, I'm wondering, is this information getting into their personalities before they even understand the rules of the game?

Interesting point here…why have rules? Rules are set for an outcome and we all know where this is leading, don't we. Why do we need an outcome, a result? Why? Because we know in our heart of hearts, we always want to win. If a parent is standing on the sidelines yelling, "You can do it, honey!" What she's really saying is, "You can win at this, honey!"

So let's quit with the façades and get down to the nitty-gritty. There are winners and losers in every game and in everyday life and that's okay, just admit it and allow it to be.

I want to make clear before going any further: I don't believe winning means you can't be gracious. I don't gloat when I put someone in their place during a competition, though I will occasionally razz a buddy out of fun. At the same time, if I lose because I make a bone-headed move, and my buddy gets the opportunity to razz me, well, I deserve it for not bringing my A-game. There are good winners and good losers and it's okay to be both at some time or other, as long you really gave the best effort you could.

•   •   •

If you find that your efforts aren't paying off when you take your game to the field, then practice. I tell my kids that when they find something in a game they feel they didn't do well in, then that's what you go to practice for, to work on the thing you need the most. If it's fielding grounders during baseball, then work on grounders at practice. You may need to work on your short game in golf, then hit buckets of balls until it is perfected. Even if it's not a sport, but perhaps a musical instrument...Drill! Drill! Drill! Practice, Practice, Practice!

Tom Brady didn't graduate with a degree in being a handsome quarterback. He had to work at it...maybe not the handsome part. Jimmy Page and Robert Plant didn't come out of high school with the song "Stairway to Heaven" written on their Trapper Keepers, and Donald Trump didn't just have his phone ring one day with someone offering him half of Manhattan. They all had to work for it.

I'm not sure if you've grasped my real concern yet. It's not necessarily about the little kids and sports, but more so about those little kids growing up to be adults who can't function in a society that can be harsh.

•   •   •

Have you ever seen a peloton in the Tour de France? When you're a cyclist in this massive group and it's moving at a good speed, it's easier to keep up than to be the guy who is trailing back and watching the peloton slip away. The further away the riders get, the harder a trailing cyclist will have to work to catch up. Oh, if only the loner had challenged himself to keep up or to stay ahead, he wouldn't be in last place. Unless there is really something physically wrong with the trailing rider, then somewhere along the way he lost focus and decided it was easier to lose than to make an effort to get back in the pack and try to win.

Try it sometime. Challenge yourself to keep up with or surpass the competition, even if you're the competition to yourself.

Who gets the big trophy at the end of a competition? Or should I ask, "Who is supposed to get the biggest trophy at the end of a competition?" The winner! That's who. Not the loser! Not second or third place! Once again, who gets the big trophy? The winner! Why? Because he put his all, his everything, into being the best and he deserves it. Tell me, who stands on the highest step after a competition in the Olympics? Who gets the gold? Not silver or bronze, but the gold?

"Well, Vincent," you say, "we can't all be the winner."

I hear you. I'm not saying that you have to be the winner in everything, but you should strive to do great. If you ran a mile in eight minutes during your last 10K run, then set your new pace to beat your best time. You don't always have to beat the competition, but you can always set a goal to beat your personal best.

When you do strive to beat your personal best, you're setting yourself up for better days ahead. You're challenging yourself to move out of complacency and be a winner. I will applaud anyone for that.

• • •

"I was the best on the team but I didn't get to play much because the coach didn't like me." Really? You mean to tell me that you were a great player and the coach liked losing more than winning, so he let you sit? People need a villain, it makes them feel better.

What could be worse than a coach that doesn't want to win? How about a helicopter parent that hovers over their kid and won't let them fail at something in order to see if the kid can muster up the strength to get back on his feet and carry through. At what point will parents let their kids deal with the challenges of life? From what I'm seeing, kids are learning to point the finger of blame.

What will the kids do when they get into the working world? Will they bring their parents in to yell at the boss on why it's not junior's fault he missed his deadlines?

You wouldn't believe how many times I've heard the "coach doesn't like me" excuse. I'm here to say that feeding on an excuse is no better than feeding on Twinkies and chocolate during a game. You're just allowing the wrong ideas to enter your brain. Why not feed on empowering ideas? Why not welcome ideas that generate energy or help to create better results? Why don't people do this? Because it appears it's easier to just accept an excuse than to have to deal with one's lack of desire or increase one's abilities.

When I look around at what's happening in the business world today, to admit that I'm upset would be a direct lie of my true feelings. I'm more pissed off than anything. Management doesn't believe they have any leverage on the employable youth. There was a time when you could fire a guy for being late, always leaving early, or playing around during company hours. Today, the younger employees come and go when they want, play on Facebook all day, and are texting their friends in the middle of meetings. Essentially they show up for a paycheck and if it doesn't satisfy them, they'll quit the job and head to the next one they see online. They'll quit that one too when the boss actually expects some real productivity. They really don't care about achieving anything on a personal level as long as they have enough for beers on the weekend, or even worse, they still live with their parents.

Why would a parent let their kids live with them as young adults? Parents are ripping away the incentive to make money. It's like being in high school again, but there is no school part. The kids have the same amount of expenses as in high school so they act as though that's where they are. The next thing you know, the kid is now forty and still living at home and guest-starring on *Ricki Lake* or *Jerry Springer*. Later in the evening they're probably surfing the Internet in their underwear.

My dad was very clear with me: "You're on your own after you graduate and there is no moving back with us." I knew I had to make it on my own. There was no free rent with mom and dad footin' the bills. And people wonder why our country is in such a slump.

I do want to give a general apology to those parents out there that are teaching their children the right way. These parents teach their kids to be respectable. They teach them to be accountable for their actions and they don't help make excuses when the child screws up. Also, to the kids out there who are not getting free handouts and have really strived to make it on their own, kudos to you for taking the initiative, I do respect that. A parent is supposed to get their child ready for the world, not be the cool babysitter.

Is there a correlation between the older generation, fifty-through-seventy-year-olds, who are having a hard time running their business that's being weighted down by employees that don't care one way or another whether they have a job or even try to better themselves? Admittedly, the older generation isn't computer-savvy and still uses the pink "while you were out" message paper jammed on a spike on the desk, whereas the younger generation has been brought up with a keyboard at their fingertips. This is the leverage of youth, but it's not as powerful as they might think. There are still young minds out there that don't have mom and dad to fall back on, and these employable youth should be the main target for the hiring management.

It just might be that hiring ex-athletes or military personnel for an aggressive position is one of the best moves any company can make. Corporate America needs to avoid kids that were raised by helicopter parents. I think business needs to take a step back and revert to some actions of the past. If an employee shows up late their pay gets docked or if they leave early they don't get paid. Every minute your computer says you were on Facebook or some other social site that isn't related to your work, you get a pop-up message that reminds you not to show up for work tomorrow.

America won't be as great as it once was if we don't turn the table and stop coddling our future with a "no one wins" attitude.

•   •   •

I could be wrong, but from my observation, there doesn't seem to be enough accountability when it comes to the kids, and the parents for that matter. When I say accountability, I'm talking about parents who rush the teacher or coach as though they've done something wrong.

There was this coach who was talking to a group of kids on a football team. The coach's tone was a bit edgy, but he was being very straightforward. He was informing the kids, teenagers at the time, that when they got to high school their mom and dad wouldn't make the decisions on who played what position and when. Everything would be based on talent and effort.

The coach let them know that rules change in high school with regards to playing time. "You might sit on the bench all season," he informed them. The message I really liked was that he started letting each kid know exactly how to improve his game, what each kid lacked while in play, and what each kid should concentrate on in practice. I had many coaches like this while growing up and it made me a better player.

Skim forward a week in the story of this coach and it continues with how a father approached him and complained that his son was picked out of the bunch. The father didn't think this was good coaching. Fast-forward and you know the outcome. The kids that didn't try, that didn't make the extra workouts, that didn't do the drills right...didn't make the starting lineup. Did the dad support the coach or blame him? I think you know the answer.

I was floored! Floored, but not surprised. There was absolutely no way this coach landed on just one kid. Hell, when I was little, there were kids who would leave the after-game huddle crying. Dads didn't come back to the coach and complain, but more often, they told their kid to step up their game. Frankly, most dads weren't at practice because they were on the clock at work. They couldn't check in via cell phone and Blackberry.

We're creating a bunch of sensitive kids who will forever grow up to be sensitive adults, unfortunately never to become real leaders.

Now, I'm certain someone out there is going to say that a real leader doesn't have to be macho and a real leader isn't macho...I agree, but come on; you can't tell me that you don't see the difference in the news as to the sensitivity of Americans on a day-in and day-out basis. It's truly having an effect on our economy as well as our common sense, not to mention our ability to sustain being a superior power in this world.

Okay, before you accuse me of being paranoid regarding any kind of superpower issues, just know, if we continue on this road we're walking, the children (future adults) of this country will be answering to a leader from another country that doesn't care about sensitivities. Have you looked around the world at all? You do know that there are countries that still cane people, right? It's interesting that these other countries haven't gone soft.

I'm not saying that we have to raise bullies, but if all you ever do is come to the aid of your child without them handling a situation for themselves, sometimes letting them learn the hard way, then our country is certainly doomed to fall.

Have you ever rescued your child from a teacher's bad grade? If you've ever heard or accepted this excuse, "It's not my fault. That teacher is failing everyone in class." If you accepted the lie, you just failed your child. Have you ever got on the coach about an after-game lecture? Have you ever rescued your child by arguing with a principle when your child was caught red-handed with something? I've heard too many stories of parents rescuing their child from a possibly great lesson.

Have you ever blamed your child's behavior on watching too many *Tom and Jerry* cartoons? Tom and Jerry aren't the parents! On a side note: Tom and Jerry may be able to teach you a lot about life and how to deal with the bullies, but your kid is going to have to grow up and learn to deal with them on his/her own.

It's one thing to help your child in a situation where adults could take advantage of them, but it's another thing to think your child could do no wrong.

I think it's good to let a kid squirm for a while when they're being held accountable for something. They should definitely have to explain their actions and why they did what they're accused of. They might actually have a legitimate excuse, but then again, if they don't, are you going to make one up for them? Teach your kid to control the situation, to be proactive and not reactive.

When a kid learns to make excuses for their actions at a young age, it's embedded in their brain that they can do this again and again. Then, if mom or dad always stands up for them, quick with an available excuse, what do they learn? Of course, they learn that excuses get you through life! As I think I pointed out, excuses from children become excuses from adults. When was the last time you saw or heard a kid really step forward and say, "I'm accountable for that, I did it." You've probably never heard it, not in this society. Don't feel so bad though, excuses also get made on a governmental level too.

•   •   •

When it comes to sports, there comes a time that a child is either playing because they enjoy the game or because they are there for their parents. Though I am into my kids' sports, if there comes a time that they don't want to play, or sit a season out, that's okay. They will have other things to do, but all in all, a kid knows when he's either outgrown the sport or feels it's okay to tell his vicariously-living parent/s that s/he's done.

I can tell which kid is in the game because he wants to be. It's usually the kid who is upset at a loss. He or she feels they could have done better, and sometimes, by the tears in their eyes, you can see they've taken the challenge personally: as an attack on their abilities. So be it! Let them feel this way. It makes for a true competitor. To stymie this type of a child is to possibly ruin a future leader of men or women. No one ever remembers second place.

I personally enjoy seeing a kid who gets involved in the game through his spirit. To me, it's so much more positive than the kids who don't care about a win or loss at all. There are kids who don't know how to lose, but more important is that the kids don't hate to lose. They're in a world where nothing really matters and as I mentioned earlier in this chapter, it shows through in their work attitude as adults.

Make no excuses, take no prisoners is the attitude we need to get back to. Be accountable for one's actions, be responsible to the guy next to you, whether you know him or not. Some people actually do live this way. They think of the affect they'll have on others before they take action. To these people...my hat is off and over my heart. They make the world a better place and we'd all do well to emulate them.

I know things are happening all over the world right now that seem bad: wars, poverty, abuse...but there is a lot of good happening also and the more we recognize someone for their actions the more we can see how easy it would be to change the bad. We need to set the example for our children so as we age and eventually leave this world we're not leaving it to unaccountable and sensitive people who don't know how to handle life.

I know it sounds like I'm grouping everyone's kids into a bleak future and there aren't going to be any leaders amongst them, but I know that's not so. I understand that kids today have different tools they'll use than my generation, but if they lack the ability to use their minds while using those tools, and I'm not talking about gaming, then this country, our world, is in for a very shaky ride.

•   •   •

Kids do grow and mature into adulthood and many will find their passion, their way in life, but I see they've often learned poorly by example and have been allowed to take things, not in stride, but at the expense of their parents who have forgotten basic principles of authority and the responsibility of parenthood: to bring up an independent, self-sufficient adult.

Perhaps I just can't see life from a kid's point of view anymore. I know I can be playful and love the experiences I'm having with my kids, but one thing is for sure: when I set a boundary, as all parents should do, if it's crossed once in contempt, I will stand strong and I will take the cell phone, their free time, their Internet service, and more.

The trophy of freedom comes with a price, whether you're a child or adult, so don't be so sensitive of my thoughts and expressions here in this book. Have a talk with yourself and ask if you've been too lenient. We all love our kids and want to give them things, but if we don't teach them truly how to earn a living, how to focus or be disciplined, then we've robbed them of the substance that make up the human spirit.

A Lost Identity

Are we lost as a country? Do we not know who we're supposed to be or if there is even an identity we're supposed to live up to? Would our forefathers be proud that they risked their lives to form a country that would eventually lose sight of its purpose? Do you even know what our country was built on?

I would be willing to bet big money that if George Washington, Thomas Jefferson, Ben Franklin, James Madison, or any of our founders were alive today and could see the mockery of what US politicians and US citizens have come to, their jaws would drop, their eyes would well up, they'd think of all the soldiers who fought for American independence from England and then realize that it seemed to be all for nothing. I think our forefathers would be appalled at our sense of entitlement and socialist approach to things.

Our forefathers brought us a land of paradise and we let vultures turn it into the land of the lost.

I would really hope that if these founding fathers were here today to witness what people have done, they'd go directly to the White House and kick the living crap out of every politician that crossed their path.

Do you sing the national anthem at the sporting events? Why? Have you betrayed your country not only through greed, but also by not being aware of what your local politician is doing? Sure, you may be the one who is speaking up but your voice is lonely and can't be heard over the nagging of the sheeple. Perhaps you weren't part of this society that bit off more than they could chew financially.

I'm not saying that our forefathers were all saints, but please understand that they sacrificed more than any other human beings this country has ever produced. They didn't die for the idea of having larger-than-life credit scores. They didn't die so oil could dominate and run our world. They didn't die so drug cartels could expand their territories. They didn't die so they could hang their heads in shame if they came back to see what people have done with their freedom.

They believed in freedom and took the biggest risk of their lives so you and I could live in this paradise away from tyranny and corrupt forces. They also believed that with freedom came enormous responsibility and unfortunately, as a society, we have forgotten that. We want freedom, we want material possessions, but we just don't want to work or take responsibility for them.

So how have we shown our appreciation to our forefathers? By having a President's Day? Or better yet, a President's Day sale? Eulogizing these great men by having a 30-percent-off sale is not only asinine, it's an abomination to their greatness. It signifies corporate greed, and the fact that people are taking part in it tells me that they aren't thinking about anyone but themselves. It's gotten so bad that people have complained about having to say the pledge of allegiance in our schools. Wouldn't you agree that there are more important things to worry or complain about?

So, I asked if you sing the national anthem. If and when you do, do you really ever stop to think or question whether you're living up to the call of freedom? Don't you want to make this a land of paradise as it was meant to be? I'll tell you, I'd want to slap silly the first person that uttered the words, "Well, I didn't ask the forefathers to do it." That's the kind of response you'd get from an immature little child and if you didn't say it, but you thought it, please grow up!

• • •

I bring freedom up because it correlates with the banking industry and the average everyday citizen. Are you in debt out your ass? Do you have five credit cards ranging with balances from $5K to $50K? Are you bitching and moaning because the banks are raising your interest rates? Didn't you read the fine print? You know they gave you the information ahead of time that they could do this or that. Why is it my responsibility to bail you out? Why is it my fault that you're a sucker?

Did you automatically assume that they were just going to be nice to you because you're nice to everyone? Are you living in reality or a fantasy land?

I can't believe the media and society claimed that the banks were using predatory business practices. So why is it the bank's fault if people bit off more than they could chew? How did they become the bad guy for your greed? Banks are about making money and though it seems they're greedy at times, realize that they can't force you to take from the pile. I'm so sick of the "I didn't know" response to everything. I sometimes wonder if people in America love to not know. How about trying this on for size: we stop making the banks out to be the bad guys, and instead, we make the people who claim "not to know" out to be the bad guys. Frankly, I think these idiots are making it worse for all of America.

If you or someone you know took out a loan on their house and bought a car, big-screen TV, or some other big-ticket item that they didn't have the money for, then they're to blame for the crisis.

How about this one: do you know someone that jammed their car loan, hot tub loan, or boat loan into their home loan? That family is now underwater and probably blaming the bank. What if they were to just admit three simple words: "I'm a sucker." At least then I might have a little respect for them.

Everyone has heard the line, "Don't live beyond your means." In case you don't understand it, "Don't spend more dollars than you earn or have." How simple is this idea? If you added up the money you're shoveling out for your credit card payments each month and then the added money for the interest you're paying…had you been patient and waited, built your savings account, you would probably have been able to buy those big-ticket items within a year. My dad used to say to me, "never be the guy that makes $100 and spends $150."

The real kick in the ass is that because you weren't patient enough to save and wait, you more than likely have a car or TV that is substandard to the latest model you could have bought.

This is not to say that if you have the job that affords you greater comforts, you shouldn't buy a car or TV, I'm just saying that you shouldn't be shoving them into loans that carry over thirty years. Sure, it's hard to save $35K for a brand-new car, but it's rather easy to pay $2K for the big-ticket item that will now cost you $12K over time (exaggeration intended).

What I'm saying is that no one in their right mind has ever thought of having a loan at 100 percent of the house value and then jamming a bunch of depreciating assets in their to boot. Once the bottom dropped out people made it sound like Wall Street bullied people into these loans. Really? Did they make you buy the new truck, hot tub, or plasma TV? What really ticks me off is that a lot of these people are getting bailed out by the government and having their bad decisions forgiven.

If you're old enough, you may remember how proud your parents were to have the money to buy their first house. Back in the day, it was hard to have credit. Our parents were proud to have the ability to buy a home. They scrimped and saved for years and years just to get the 10 percent or 20 percent down payment. People used to be proud to say they earned the right to own a home. They didn't fudge on the loan papers, filling in the blanks with unscrupulous realtors, declaring that they made more than they did.

I don't want to believe that people were getting "no verification loans" where they didn't have to verify their income or produce statements regarding their assets. The joke is that they really thought this was going to work out well.

When a bank looked at your parents' loan they didn't offer them $50K more just to add to the amount of interest that could be charged.

I laugh when people say they took the extra money so they could pay off their credit card's high interest rates and by rolling them into the home loan they're saving huge amounts of interest. Sure they are! They're saving it right up to the point of realization that the credit cards now have a zero balance and can now be used to purchase new things. Sure they are! Right up to the point that they realize the interest they're now paying on the home loan with the added money is going to be paid on for a longer term than it would be to have just paid off the cards. It might take seven years to pay off a card, but that's just seven, not thirty.

Are people really that dumb? Unfortunately, actions speak louder than words. If this is you that I'm talking about, and you do know if it is, take some of your cards and cut them up. Take the others and put them in a bowl of water, then put that bowl in the freezer. If you want to buy something you'll have to wait for the defrosting and hopefully you'll change your mind by that time. Perhaps you'll then be able to admit that you can't afford what you had your ill-fated hopes on.

"Well, my house will go up in value and I'll be able to sell it for a profit." Sure you can! Good luck with that. It may take another ten years to get the housing market back up to where it was.

We know banks aren't about occupying office space. They're about making money and they do it through the selling of loans to the public. They must make a good return on the risk. I've taken loans throughout my lifetime and they've always offered me more than I needed, sometimes up to five times the amount. Did I ever take the offer? NO! I was prudent and made good decisions. I'm also prudent and buy insurance…oops, we'll get to that later. You have to use your brain and take some accountability and responsibility. Don't let your brain write a check that your finances can't cover. If you do write that check, don't blame everyone else for your stupidity.

Banks understand that there's a sucker born every minute. If in case you don't know who the sucker is, if you've done any of the aforementioned, that sucker is YOU! Man, I'd love to negotiate against you or play poker with you. Give me a call if you have money burning a hole in your pocket.

In case you didn't know this next tidbit of information, I want to be the nice guy and help you figure something out regarding your credit card. If you have a balance due date and you wait to make your payment just before it's due, you're losing a lot of money throughout the year. You're paying more in interest than you have to. As soon as you get your bill, pay it! The lag time you've been doing is still accruing interest whereas if you pay it immediately, the accruing stops until your next statement. This isn't a brain teaser…it's pretty easy to understand.

Learn the game that banks play with your money so one day you can stand proud in the middle of Washington, DC, and let our forefathers know you're doing right by them. Hell, you don't even have to go to DC, you can thank them from your kitchen chair by silent prayer.

Years ago, the government's opinion was said something to the effect of, "We need to make it so everyone can buy a house. That's the American dream." Well, that's not the American dream. The way it was originally said was like this, "Everyone has the right to have the opportunity to buy a house." This is a far cry from "everyone should be in a house." Putting people in houses just for the sake of filling space and getting the numbers up isn't conducive to running a well-organized country. Again, people were getting into houses that they just couldn't afford, all because someone thinks that it's the American dream.

God forbid anyone should point their finger at the government for pushing people into a bad spot. I hope we never hear, "It's the American dream for everyone to drive a Ferrari."

While I'm at it, I want to emphasize how F'd-up it is that the government sold their mortgage-forgiving plan to the American public. I've heard of more people who have gotten their mortgage plan cut in half and now get the government's super-low interest rate. What are the people doing with all the extra money they save with daddy G's help? They're not paying things off as much as they're buying more debt-loading goods. Sooner or later these people won't be able to pay the government mortgage either.

I pay my bills on time and if I was in a bind I'd get my ass out to wash cars or pull weeds...anything to cover my bills on my terms. Have some dignity, some integrity. Here it is, I always pay for the things I want or need and I do it on time each month. My interest rates never get lowered and my mortgage wasn't even considered to be refinanced by the government. I went to do my own refinancing because lowering your interest rate makes good business sense. I didn't do it from a bailout, but even then, with as good as my credit is: I had to damn near give blood and urine samples.

What do Americans who own their homes dream of? Paying the damn thing off! That's what! They often dream of never having gotten into the home in the first place... especially now that the properties are upside down on the loan. I guess someone decided the American dream should be shot full of holes and the government is the one taking aim.

Trying to jam the American dream down everyone's throats has come close to actually ruining the American dream for those who actually understand the dream and deserve it. Weird, huh?

Again, the opportunity to own a home is not the same as jamming someone of lesser means in a place that will outpace the meager means they have. If you want to do better by them, buy them a freakin' tent and force them to save money for a down payment on something with brick and mortar.

The government needs the housing market to continue to move forward. They need the industry to pick up and thrive so new homes will be built: putting people/contractors back to work...which helps to move the economy.

Let me lay it out for you. The fact that the government did their best to jam everyone into a home is now crushing the economy.

Regardless of good or bad credit, people are able to get into a house. Regardless of the economy and the absence of good, stable, quality jobs, the government still wants to loan money, to increase profit through interest, to let people be in debt out their ass—but hey, they've got a home.

So you might ask, what does this have to do with identity? People are identifying themselves as successful if they can say that they own their home. They try to create an identity through the cars they drive or the big-ticket items they buy. All of this is crap because the moment anyone defaults on their payments and loses their house or car, they're still the same person they were, but now they're broke and usually embarrassed. Frankly, I'm not sure if they're truly embarrassed because by being so, that would mean that they're taking responsibility for their decisions.

•   •   •

Americans have lost their identity when it comes to valuing things. When I was a kid I learned what value meant. I was never just handed a gold or platinum card and told, "Have fun, kid." In today's times, kids aren't taught the value of things, to have pride in your work in order to make one's desires come true. It's really a placid life for many of the younger generation. I'm not going to feel sorry for them when the limit is breached, the parents are out of work, and the kid comes home to bitch and moan about how the card was declined and they can't have their unearned things. Hey, kids, go get a paper route, mow some grass, start a lemonade stand. Would it kill you to make some cash to pay for that new iPod or video game?

It's only because of the debacle regarding the housing crisis that the banks are now making a comeback to the proper way of loaning money. It's about time. Yet, now that the stakes are higher for one to get and keep credit, we still have a society crying about how things aren't fair.

What society isn't realizing is that things are now becoming fair. Business is being done the way it was originally supposed to be done. If you aren't credit-worthy of a certain level or amount, you don't get it. If they lower your available credit as you pay down your balance, good for them. They're just straightening out the mess they helped to create, but not without the public carrying their share of the load.

• • •

The government has lost its identity by trying to be all things to everyone. They want to bail out this company or that company. They don't want anyone to fail and this hurts society as a whole. Look at it this way: A child looks up to his or her parent and understands the role of authority. The parents who give their child everything fail that child. The parent loses the respect and position of authority and the child learns how to manipulate the parent anytime they want. It's prevalent with many trust-fund babies: kids that grew into adults but never had to work for anything, so eventually they fail because they don't know how to earn or place value on things. Nowadays, kids think that their parents' wealth is their income. They started on third base, but believe that they hit a home run. They're delusional!

Capitalism is supposed to have a winner-and-loser mentality, but here are parents in the twenty-first century teaching children that winning doesn't matter, as the parents struggle to cover the bills.

Do you see where I'm going with this? I know I covered it in a previous chapter, but it's relevant to bring it up again and again. You must see the correlation and do more than just shake your head and say something stupid like, "Well that's just the way it's done," or, "I'm just one person. What can I do?"

The truth of what you can do is to fight back and find your identity, let your kids know that there is a new marshal in town and there are going to be some new guidelines to be met.

Okay, you might say, "Well, my kids aren't like that. I'm not wealthy and they don't get everything at their every whim." Still, I tell you, take a serious look around and look at their actions. Are they lacking in grades? Is their bedroom a mess yet they have the latest video game on the market? Have they ever said, "Whatever!" If so, then you're not receiving the respect that should have been present all along. You've lost your identity as a role model and as a parent. Trust me when I tell you that your kids will grow and wish they had done things differently and also wish that you had raised them with a much more disciplined life.

It's not 1950 anymore and I don't believe in spanking, using a belt, or any of the old-school ways. I don't judge people who do believe in it, I just don't feel the need to go there in that frame of mind. I do, however, believe in real discipline and I believe the American people want some control again.

There was an incident in Singapore in 1994 and President Clinton had to be called in. Why it was any of his business is beyond me. A young man named Michael

Fay from the US had vandalized some property and was eventually caught. The punishment was to be four whacks with a rattan rod, a serious caning. It was front-page news until OJ Simpson's long drive on the 405 freeway in southern California stole the show.

When polls were taken, it turned out that most Americans agreed with the caning process. Many from Michael's home town called in to support the caning and expressed how tired they were of America's lax and apologetic attitude toward criminals: giving them more rights than the victims they subjected to humility.

I'm not saying to take a cane to your kids, but I'm saying that we should not let the inmates run the asylum. I think there are many who would agree.

Singapore had no problem with the world viewing them as authoritarian and decisive in actions. Their identity was that of our past history: steal a horse and you will be hung. Funny how the message rang out throughout the world that Singapore wasn't the place to screw around and break the law.

Would I want this to happen to one of my kids? Of course not, but at the same time that I may not want it, I understand that rules are in place and if one decides to break them, so be the consequences...my child or not.

I sure would like to know what Michael Fay thinks to this day about the caning. I would hope he'd admit that it was a just punishment for his actions and that he kept his nose clean from that point on.

Perhaps if kids were shown movies of what happens to criminals in other countries, they'd thank their lucky stars that they're in America where it's more like a pillow fight or being whipped with a wet noodle.

America has lost its identity and other countries are now pointing and using us as an example, saying, "See what happens when you become soft, you get repeat offenders and the punishments are a joke to those who commit the crimes."

Of course, other countries aren't saying anything we don't already know, but we're also not doing anything to prove them wrong...because they're not wrong and because our country doesn't know how to react to the reality of a winner-less society.

So what do we do as a society to get an identity that resonates with the rest of the world? We do a 180-degree turnaround and learn to become the nation we once were.

Some might think that we've become more intelligent and that smart people don't resort to violence as a way of settling problems. Well, if you believe that then you have no right backing a war in the Middle East because truth be known, that's as violent as it gets. Sometimes you have to fight for what's important.

As a country, we need to go back to teaching our youth that it's okay to win. It can be taught with a maturity that one should not gloat, unless it's all in a sarcastic and fun way, but teach them that winning is expected and giving 100 percent of your effort is required.

In order to recapture our identity we need to make laws less bendable and less easily manipulated by attorneys. This means that just because Joe Shmoe has millions of dollars doesn't mean he gets better treatment than the guy who must use a public defender. Evidence that doesn't get admitted in a court of law is proof that a victim is not getting represented fairly.

Identity requires that we enforce strictly those things that make us a united society. Why are we letting our leaders break the Constitution of the United States and make a mockery of the founding fathers that gave us an identity the world recognized as powerful and proud?

The world is sitting back and watching America go through conflict after conflict within its own ranks. They watch a country divided by two parties who constantly bad-mouth each other like two little children fighting over a toy in a sandbox, only the toy happens to be our new identity...failure!

What Happened to Thunder Road?

Have you ever noticed that real music no longer appears to exist? Everyone is vying to be the next American Idol (AI), but no one really wants to work for it. Unlike Billy Joel, who had to take up boxing because he kept getting beat up for being the kid in a NY neighborhood taking piano lessons and walking around with music books under his arm. He did what it took to make his talent complete and make his dreams come true. He's the true American Idol.

On a side note: Why can we get millions of people to vote on *American Idol*, but have to beg people to vote for a president?

Young people may show up at the audition of *AI* and if chosen as a contestant they'll have to compete, but that's really nothing like what the legends of music had to do. Artists like the Beatles, the Eagles, Billy Joel, Led Zepplin, AC/DC, Aerosmith, Mötley Crüe, Journey, Kiss, Van Halen, Guns N' Roses, the Rolling Stones, Bon Jovi, and Bruce Springsteen went out and made themselves known by the sheer love of what they did and people couldn't help but to fall in love with their music.

By the way, these bands made it when there was no such thing as Twitter, Facebook, or MySpace to spread the word. The word got around because these musicians earned the right to play for the crowds.

They all started out the same way: they had an instrument in front of them and they picked out a couple of chords, sometimes by accident, and eventually found a sound that they could make into their own.

Some of the biggest names got their asses kicked as kids because they may have played the piano or some wind instrument. They may not have been considered cool as children, but they worked through their embarrassing moments and found that getting their ass kicked for the love of their life was worth every bit of the pain.

Today, kids want to go on TV and be adored by Americans everywhere. They think that because they can play Guitar Hero that they'd be good as real musicians. They don't do the work that could make them icons. As a matter of fact, most of the "Idols" never make it in the business past their first year after winning.

Big music corporations are taking these naive kids and telling them they can be this or that. Big music industry knows that they will find someone with a good voice, have a songwriter create lyrics, oftentimes using original music from big-named talent, throw a back-up band into a recording session, and mix it until out from the other end is a one-hit wonder waiting to happen. It's weird! It seems like the roles have been reversed. Back in the day, the bands worked like crazy to get the attention of the record companies. Now, the record companies are inventing talent…if you want to call it that.

After that record hits the top of the charts, because there isn't anyone else able to spend like big music industry, they see if they can keep using the same singer, but if that fails, they go out and find the next cute things that looks good in front of a microphone.

Hate to burst those music bubbles out there, but truly, this is what's happening. It's all synthesized crap. I can't even hear a guitar in most songs on the radio. If there is a guitar in the background it's because there is a riff from an old song being used in the new song. It even sounds like the voices are synthetic. There are more songs sounding like T-Pain and an auto-tuner effects processor. Now people don't even need to sing or have good voices, they just let the computer do the work.

On a side note: It's gotten so crazy out there that the big bands are doing reality-type shows in order to find their next lead singer. Real groups don't want to depend on voice-altering computers for their lead vocals. INXS found a guy through a TV show. Journey found their lead singer off of YouTube. The music world is turning into the Mark Wahlberg movie *Rock Star*.

Where are the bands that travel in a van from town to town creating original music? Go do yourself a favor and watch the Bruce Springsteen documentary on the making of the *Born to Run* album. Check out how long it took. Check out how much emotion and time went into the music. See how many times they changed a song around, changed the arrangements, or changed the solos. Take the time to really listen to the stories behind the songs...that's where the real music happens.

Again, where are the bands that travel in a van from town to town creating original music? Where is my Thunder Road?

If you can recall standing in line for an LP or the latest CD to be released by your favorite artist, then you're old enough to understand how the big music industry has ruined the art of song.

Napster was one of the first Internet sites to let anyone download music for free. It ripped off millions of dollars and also stole the ability for the younger generation to understand the word "anticipation."

No one waits any more. You may ask, "Why should they?" Well, because of the old Chinese proverb, "Good things come to those who wait!" Even if it's not Chinese, the truth remains.

There really are some things that technology has spoiled, and music and movies are two of them. Technology plus the lack of anticipation equals a lot of bad movies. Why don't we have more great movies like *The Shawshank Redmeption*, *The Godfather*, *The Usual Suspects*, *Rocky*, *A Few Good Men*, *Wall Street*, *Pulp Fiction*, *Goodfellas*, *Taxi Driver*, *Raiders of the Lost Ark,* and *Star Wars*?

"How did technology spoil movies?"

Both the music and movie industry are about making big dollars in very little time. The movie industry has taken hold of the children's market and creates a ton of crap that pacifies a kid for an hour or so, but really doesn't care about doing a good job. They will hire out production companies and insist on the work being done in two months for something that would normally take six.

Unfortunately, most viewers either don't care or don't understand what is going on behind the scenes. Who gives a rat's ass as long as their child is slightly entertained for an hour or so. The storylines are usually agendas for the environmentalists and offer nothing of substance that we aren't barraged with on a daily basis as it is. It's the same with teen and adult movies; they seem to pump out movie after movie without attention to script.

There have been so many remakes of *Frankenstein* or the F'n werewolf that Hollywood has completely lacked the ability to create stories that are of character. I read the other day that there are over seventy-five remakes slated for Hollywood production in the year 2010. To top it off, a new version of *The Karate Kid* and *The A-Team* just came out! Hence, this is the reason that most films that win the big awards are made by independent film producers—people who care about story content that engages human emotions everywhere. There are over a quarter million scripts written and pitched to top executives every year and all anyone can produce is a remake. That statistic in itself is shameful. Wake up, Hollywood!

So I ask, "Why are the prices for movie tickets going up when the value of what you get has gone down?" If you want to see great movies, go rent one from your local Blockbuster, one that was made in the fifties or sixties and is usually in black and white. Believe it or not, you'll really see the difference in the quality of the movies comparatively, the acting and the storylines. Are there any good movies today? Sure, but very few with a storyline that will grab your heart and wrench it to tears.

The anticipation factor is gone via the road of technology. I believe that people need to stand back and be aware of what they're purchasing and what value it will really add to their lives. If no real value is added, don't waste the money.

The addictions of the gimme gimme society is eroding the entertainment field. Well, what happens when the day comes that there is no more material for the addiction? Even a true-to-life junky loses interest in their drug and finds another way to stay high. People want everything this very moment and technology has delivered. This can lead to poor judgment with a result of too many irreversible mistakes. Learn to wait. Look for your Thunder Road.

Gone are the days of the next Rolling Stones. They've been tested against time and all of the changes in music: hard rock, grunge, rap, pop, techno...and the world still flocks to see them. Who will be the next Billy Joel, Madonna, or Aerosmith? Tell me which artists from today will be selling out arenas in twenty or thirty years. Groups that used to speak about real emotions or situations that people understand are marked by an era as if in shame. "Oh, thank god the eighties are over"? Bullshit! Bring 'em back!

Little does the younger generation realize that true rock and roll has a place in the lives of millions; it's an industry that is being held onto by the diehards. My hat is off to those garage bands that still believe they can make great music. These bands are few and far between and are headed up by musicians that can hear the difference between a real instrument and one that is computer generated. You will rarely find these bands in the big venues anymore. No, more than likely you have to go to a local bar or a street fair of some type.

Bands like Nickelback and Foo Fighters are probably some of the last bands to play rock and roll with any clear understanding of what "the road" means. I'm sure there are a few others, but the numbers dwindle as each year passes.

It appears to me that country music has more talented entertainers with an ability to play an instrument while storytelling than all of the other venues combined. Perhaps the country genre is the last great place a band can still be created and creative. Listen to Tim McGraw, Keith Urban, and Kenny Chesney, and you'll hear stories. These stories not only take you back to a special time in your life that makes you smile, but they also get you to think. That's the value of country music, it's real.

So, again, I ask you, where is the next Joe Cocker, Bob Dylan, Tom Petty, Willie Nelson, George Straight, Styx, or any other of the great artists that didn't wait for their fate to be determined by a panel of three judges with less than a track record of road experience.

Simon Cowell may have helped shape modern pop music, but into what, is the question. As for Randy Jackson, he put his chops in as a bass guitarist, but there may be something to the fact that he no longer is on the road with Journey and has lost his touch. Come on, Randy, pick up that guitar and play for the people like you used to. Show them that you still have some talent.

What I'm getting at here is that the younger generation is not business-savvy enough to get where they need to be. They build their hopes that talent alone will get them by. I guess that makes me a panelist when I say, NEXT!

If the music industry is going to change, to be something more than it is at present, then someone will need to come along and teach these kids how to take the time and do things right. Interesting note here: unless someone with experience is willing to give a kid something, and give it right now, then a kid has no option but to play the game at a pace more conducive to true success.

I've said it before and I'll say it again: In another ten years these kids aren't going to know how to do anything and they'll all claim to have attention deficit disorder (ADD). They're going to be scatterbrained idiots if they don't slow down and learn to anticipate the future.

Turn That Thing Off!

When I was a kid and the newest gadget was being released, I waited in anticipation. The Walkman was the very first version of the iPod, except it didn't have all the bells and whistles. You could take the Walkman anywhere and listen to your favorite tunes, though you couldn't download anything because there weren't sites to do such things and the computer was just being introduced to society.

Remember how great the Walkman was? You only listened to one cassette at a time and you actually had to rewind the song when it ended. The anticipation of hearing the song again seemed to make it better.

When my friends, who are older than me, were kids, they used to have record players and big stereo systems. Parents used to yell down the hall, "Turn that damn thing off!" Well, times haven't changed much.

Today it's cell phones, Blackberries, iPods, computers, video games, electronic books, giant TVs with surround sound, and a number of other gadgets that create a separation of family. Now I'm not saying that I want to be like the town in the movie *Footloose*, but I do think we've become a distracted society that is always being hurried.

I do use a cell phone for work, and trust me when I tell you I am that annoying guy you see around town. I'm on the cell like crazy during business hours. I wear the headset, I carry a cell phone, an iPad, a Blackberry, a laptop, and more. It makes me want to kick my own ass. However, it gets turned off the moment I get home. Friends often joke about me because when they want to talk with me on the weekends, they can't. I turn the damn thing off!

I use the technology to make money and to stay connected, not to get disconnected from my family. Have you ever noticed how many people are on their cell phones and texting while they're driving? Have you ever gone to a game and noticed how many people are busy on their iPhones and not watching the game? Go to a concert and you'll see a good number of people on their cell. Go to a college campus and find me one kid not on a device while walking around campus. What the hell is going on? Can't people enjoy a little time away from the phone anymore?

Dinner used to be a sacred part of a family's day. Now, you can go to a restaurant and watch a man sitting with his family while talking to his buddy on the cell. The family is completely ignored and believe it or not, respect is out the door. I even see kids that are texting while sitting at a meal with their parents. This is absolute crap! Turn that damn thing off! More times than not, I notice families out for dinner and everyone is on some sort of "device." It makes me want to punt that device right out the door. I think things have gone too far.

You want to know why so many kids don't have good communication skills these days? Because all they do is text in abbreviations and don't pay attention to how it carries over into their speaking habits. A guy I know, who is in his early twenties, is a magician with his cell phone. He can drive while texting, eating, and changing radio stations.

Even during school the kids are texting each other. They don't need to see their little keyboard, they have it memorized. It's not so funny that they can text without looking as it is deplorable that they're doing this in place of actual learning while in class.

What if they spent their time in class learning about the things they're truly going to need, like economics?

Turn that damned thing off during school hours. If there's a real problem where the kids need to be contacted, a parent can call the school and have the child removed from class.

Truth of the matter, kids and adults alike believe they're missing out on something when they don't have a hand on their phone or other communication device. Ask yourself what you're really missing. Is it that important to have Facebook or Twitter downloaded to our phone so you can know that a friend is doing their laundry or needs a cow for their Farmville application? Have you ever noticed that the people who claim to be the busiest are the ones on Facebook all day?

Whatever happened to privacy? Does everyone want to be so famous that they Tweet all day long about absolute bullshit! Is your life so wrapped up in what the celebrity of the day is doing that your world stops if they are having lunch somewhere a thousand miles away from you? How unproductive can our society get with all of this social media crap?

Though I understand the positive uses regarding social media, I'm thinking the bad far outweighs the good. Yes, one can spread the word of a certain club or activity that may interest others. I know of a few authors that use it in the release of their latest work. It can be a mountain of worth to raise funds for earthquake victims in another country. I get all that, but really, "I'm doing my laundry." "I'm taking out the trash." "I can't wait to watch *Lost* or *24* tonight." Turn that damn thing off!

Whatever happen to the anticipation of things? Technology kicked anticipation in the groin and it's not getting up. It's a sad state of affairs when people won't appreciate the idea of anticipation. I remember waiting for the latest album by my favorite band to be delivered in the local store. I remember waiting in long lines for tickets to see the next great movie. Now, you can download music instantly to your iPod, purchase movie tickets before leaving your home, and pirate movies before they're released. Back in the day, there was anticipation in regards to sex and nudity. Now kids are being caught sending body shots over their cell phones. Turn the damn thing off!

I use a Blackberry for work and at the end of the workday, if I'm home, the phone goes off. When I'm done for the day, it means I'M DONE. No one—not from my office, not my clients—will get a message through to me. I work hard for a living and there comes a time in the day that my life is mine.

Can you believe that there used to be a time when, if a senior boss was out of the office and the second in charge couldn't get a hold of them, then the second in charge would actually have to make a command decision? It's incredible to think that the world used to actually run somewhat smoothly without the technology of the day. Amazing!

When technology invades your personal life, you're out of balance. Try this little experiment: Set the cell phone down and go take a long walk. Go to the park with your spouse. Swing on the swings with your kids. Leave the cell in the car and go play some basketball with your buddies. Learn what anticipation is all about. Just think of the million missed calls you'll get to return when you get back home or into your car. I wonder how many people go to bed each night and when placing their head on their pillow they're quickly reminded that their Bluetooth is still connected to their ear.

You know you have a serious problem if you can sleep with your Bluetooth still in place. If this is really what you do, please...get some help. FYI, you'll never be as important as you think you are.

I think a lot of this technology has worked against kids today. They are so used to instantaneous results that they just expect everything to appear in seconds. They don't understand the real work it takes to receive good things. They're a gimme gimme group and if they can't press a send button then it must not really exist. The kids of this day in age are being dumbed down by a technology that on the outside looks to be the next wave of future jobs, but if that job doesn't pay a cool million, the kids won't want it because it doesn't happen as instantly as they're used too.

Tell me what happens to a dumbed-down society, one that has no concept of how things truly work. If you can't tell me, I'll tell you. What happens is this: your kids will depend on you until the day you die. If you've ever seen the movie *Surrogates*, with Bruce Willis, you'll know what I mean. Sure the technology was incredible, but it took society to a new level of shame. No one wanted to be themselves. No one knew how to be themselves.

This movie actually makes me nervous because I don't think it's that far off from what could happen in our society. Do you recall the technology scenes in *Minority Report?* We're not that far off from there either. What about the movie *Enemy of the State?* Big brother is watching in more ways than you know.

Going back to Facebook, you ever notice how some people have a thousand friends or more? You can't possibly make me believe for one second that people have one thousand close friends. I actually think that the more people one has on one's Facebook page, the fewer real friends one has. I believe that people are using Facebook to create friends so they can feel better about themselves. Again, I understand the fan page for celebrities, but the regular John Smith knowing each and every person on his page is a farce—yet, how lucky they are to know what he had for lunch.

Anyone that wants to get to know me on a level of what I'm doing at any given moment or whether I have a load of laundry going or that I'm heading to the gym, well, they need to get a life. Somewhere in all of this are some really insecure people that desperately need friends, regardless of whether they know them.

If you're signing on people as friends that you don't even know or know how they came to you, it makes no real sense and I'm glad you're not my friend. Why don't you get to know yourself, or better yet, take out your real friends and get to know them better. Go be a real friend instead of adding people to a page that looks more like a pyramid scheme.

You may not like what I just said, but please, don't shoot the messenger, texter, emailer, app user, game player, or whatever the hell anyone who sends a message these days is called.

Pick up a guitar, sit at the piano, go hit some golf balls, visit the batting cages, and explore the world you may have known long before your venture into cyberspace. Hell, take a singing lesson and be your own American Idol.

More and more Americans are momentarily using the computer to find places like Meetup.com where they can join groups that are shutting off the computer and living beyond the proverbial box.

Turn that damn thing off! Go out and explore the world.

Attack of the Vampires

My wife had been shopping at Target one day and while walking through the parking lot to her car, she witnessed another driver backing out from a space and right into the rear of her car. It was no big deal: no air bags, no injuries, no severe damage, and the proper information was exchanged. The interesting part of the scenario came a week or so later when my wife got a package in the mail from a personal injury firm. To be honest, the package was downright impressive. There was a letter to inform us that they knew of this accident from the police report. Included were all kinds of glossy brochures that let us know how much they cared for our safety and our rights. They were even willing to visit us in our home to discuss the incident. Obviously, everything would be free unless we won the case they would present. They mentioned all the cash and benefits we'd get from having a case and how easy it is as most cases are settled out of court.

The brochures listed all of the success stories, and to be truthful, it crossed my mind that I might want to contact these people, file a lawsuit and win millions. Then that damn little angel shows up on my shoulder and keeps my ethics in check. My point is this: some lawyers are out there making it seem like everyone is doing it. They're over-encouraging people to sue.

We all know what the job of an attorney is: sue for as much money as possible and win. There are a ton of attorneys that really are honest and fight for a good cause, both on the business front and the personal sector. Then there are the ambulance chasers, the guys who see only dollar signs and are willing to bend rules to crank up the possible payout. I'm all for making a buck until it starts to move our society into a state of the acceptance of lawsuits. Just like everything else, this whole "Let's sue for millions" phenomenon used to not exist.

I think there needs to be a law that if you sue a corporation for millions of dollars because you did something that you shouldn't have, if you lose, you have to pay the corporation and its lawyers. How great would it be if there was actually skin in the game on both sides? What if the lawyers had to pay for a loss? Would they still chase the big payday just to see if they could win?

There are no repercussions for frivolous law suits and I think it's flat-out wrong. Every ladder that is sold across the United States has a warning attached to it that tells the user to not stand above a certain level or step, yet there are idiots out there who insist on using their ladder incorrectly; they hurt themselves and then sue the ladder company, usually winning. What a scam!

These frivolous lawsuits happen in so many ways, all day and every day. Two people get in a minor traffic accident of less than 10 mph and the next thing you know, one of them is wearing a neck brace. It's like the courtroom scene in a *Brady Bunch* episode: Mr. Brady slams a book to the ground behind the defendant to draw a reaction and prove that the neck brace is a hoax, a big scammer who is seeking money they don't deserve.

Of course, there are hoops to jump through before one actually gets any money. They must visit a practicing doctor for a period of time and in many cases, not truly being injured, they're now compromising their integrity. I guess it's good to know how much integrity costs these days.

The $25K the person gets is nothing compared to the rewards the doctors and lawyers are getting. I guess it doesn't take much for some people to sleep well at night. I don't think I could sleep after swindling anyone out of money that wasn't truly deserved. Does anyone care about karma anymore? Everyone should watch the TV show *My Name Is Earl*.

It seems that people have an idea that big companies are making so much money that it's easy or okay to scam them. I guessing that maybe it's because the big bad corporation doesn't have a face so it feels like the everyday person taking it to *the man*. It sounds a bit similar to our talk on taxes— "the rich have so much that it's okay to take it from them."

Isn't it oddly funny that people will not work harder to give themselves a better life and they have no problem taking from someone that has done the work it takes to get ahead.

The woman who won millions of dollars from a fast food chain…are her fingertips not working? Couldn't she tell by touching the cup of coffee that it was HOT! Now, if she had ordered four breakfast sandwiches for herself and the employee only gave her three, then they started to fight and the employee had intentionally thrown a scalding hot cup of coffee in her face, I could understand a lawsuit. If a scene had gone down like this I would expect and support a lawsuit. Wait! Stop! Check that…I'm actually not really sure I would support that lawsuit; after all, the employee was doing a good thing by lowering her breakfast intake by two thousand calories. Maybe he should sue her. It's a shame that companies have to have different forms of liability insurance for this very reason.

There was something I read not too long ago: a person was suing her work because there was another employee that was farting too much. She was offended. Really? Offended so much that they had to sue? I'm glad I didn't grow up with this person. My friends and I would have been sued all day and every day. By the way, I bet this lawsuit happy employee wasn't very good at their job…just a hunch.

I love it when someone sues the big tobacco companies. At what point did they think that inhaling smoke thirty-five times a day for fifty years was okay to do? Were these people really shocked that their lungs stopped working? I'd like to see any company get to sue those people who used to work for them, but took time away because of sickness from smoking, not to mention the smoke breaks. That would be awesome. Can I sue the people who are standing and smoking outside a public building? I find myself having to hold my breath when I enter or exit a building. Can I sue the guy sitting next to me on the train for smelling too much like cigarette smoke and cologne?

One of the most commonly heard-of lawsuits is probably when someone finds a hair in their food. If I found a hair,

I might, at the very most, expect my meal to be comped. Not everyone's meal, just mine.

People have done so many things in their lives that they could be grossed out about, but when a small hair gets in their food the world ends? Come on...some of you...think where your mouths have been. Many of these people are the same ones that lick their fingers to turn a page, make out with their pets, or chew on their nails.

When it comes to finding things in your food that just aren't a part of the recipe, for example, a finger, I might be a little more disgusted, but if that finger had a nice diamond ring attached to it, case closed. I'm heading to the nearest diamond appraiser I can find.

Every thirty seconds in this country there is a lawsuit filed on behalf of someone who feels hurt in some way, shape, or form. Like the idiots in other chapters, these people aren't the ones we'll be going to when we want to set precedence of the words "ethics" or "responsible."

A man sued Busch Gardens when he pushed open a bathroom stall door. The door swung back and cracked him in his head.

A man sued Disneyland because he fainted from embarrassment when the ride attendant confronted him as he was waiting in the shortcut line for a ride.

A women sued Wendy's after finding a finger in her chili. It turns out that the woman placed the finger in her food and was trying to scam the fast food chain.

A woman visiting the local aquarium with her family sued the city of Norwalk after her child stepped in dog poop just outside of the garage building.

A forty-three-year-old woman sued Sacramento State University after losing the race for Homecoming Queen.

A man sued a family for mental distress after being locked in their garage for over a week. He was trying to rob the home while the family was on vacation.

A man sued pro basketball player Michael Jordan because he said Michael Jordan looked like him and people all over the place would approach him. He sued MJ and the founder of Nike, Phil Knight, for over $800 million dollars.

A woman sued McDonald's because she spilled their hot coffee all over herself which resulted in third-degree burns.

A man sued a strip club because he claimed he suffered from whiplash.

A woman sued her TV network for making wrong weather predictions, causing her to catch a cold.

A woman sued a movie theater because she suffered from emotional distress after watching a horror movie.

A convicted bank robber on parole entered a bank and robbed it. The stolen money had a tear gas device installed that worked. The robber sued the bank.

A guy was involved in a car collision. He sued the drivers of the truck that were responsible for the crash. He stated that from then on, his sexual relationship with his wife went downhill and he was unable to maintain their sex life. He said that the accident turned him into a homosexual. He won his case and was awarded $200,000, while his wife received $25,000.

A woman had a friend give her a haircut. Unhappy with her new look the woman sued him for $75,000.

A college student decided to "moon" someone from his dorm-room window that was on a high floor. He lost his balance and fell out of his window. He sued saying he was not warned of the dangers of living on the high floor.

A woman was awarded $80,000 by a jury after breaking her ankle by tripping over a child who was running inside a furniture store. The store owners were shocked by the verdict since the running child was hers.

A young man won $74,000 plus medical expenses when his neighbor ran over his hand with his car. The young man didn't realize the owner was in the driver seat and waiting to leave when he decided to steal his neighbor's hubcaps.

A woman was awarded by a jury that a restaurant pay her $113,500 after she slipped on a spilled soda and broke her tailbone. The soda was on the floor because the woman had thrown it at her boyfriend thirty seconds earlier during an argument.

An older woman purchased a new motor home. She set the cruise control at 70 mph and left the driver's seat to go to the back and make herself a sandwich. The motor home left the freeway, crashed, and overturned. The woman sued the motor home maker for not putting in the owner's manual that she couldn't actually leave the driver's seat while the cruise control was set. The jury awarded her $1,750,000 PLUS a new motor home. The motor home company actually changed their manuals as a result of this suit.

A woman in Delaware sued the owner of a night club because she fell from the bathroom window to the floor and knocked out her two front teeth. The woman was trying to sneak into the club through the window to avoid paying the entrance fee of $3.50. She was awarded $12,000.

A man in prison sued to play Dungeons & Dragons in jail. He was serving a lifetime jail sentence for murder.

A woman sued Google because she was hit by a car while walking on a road that Google maps suggested.

•   •   •

I don't know that I buy every single one of these to be true. I can somehow believe that they've been stretched from the truth by a margin or so, but I don't doubt that people actually sue over the dumbest of their own errors. Everyone knows the one about the woman spilling extremely hot coffee on herself and winning millions. I sometimes wonder if other people caught wind of these types of lawsuits and tried to make up their own little accident.

Anyway, it just goes to show you, America needs some help and apparently there's always a vampire attorney available for just such a case. There needs to be some ramifications to lawsuits that are frivolous. I'm sure someone is asking, "How do you know that they're really frivolous? Maybe that person really was hurt?"

This is a good and honest question. The truth is that most people know when they're putting on an act for the money and so does the attorney handling the case. There needs to be some skin involved in all lawsuits. If you bring a lawsuit against someone or some company and they have a more solid case than you, if you do lose, again, you pay them.

If the average wage earner knew that he was going to spend the next ten years paying off a lawsuit he never should have filed, I'd hope they'd think twice.

I don't know how many Friday nights my family and I have sat down to watch a movie while eating pizza. Have you ever taken a bite of pizza that was so hot it stuck to the roof of your mouth? I have, over and over again. Each time I do, my wife looks at me and laughs. When will I ever learn? Do I go out to sue the pizza company for giving me hot food that I ordered? NO! Do I suffer the consequences of the roof of my mouth being instantly melted and tenderized by heat? YES! Will I ever learn? Probably not, but I still eat my lawsuit-free pizza.

I like lawyers and there's a lot of great ones, I even have friends that I call vampires because there job is to suck the blood out of the entity they're suing. It seems that everyone thinks these big corporations are just made of money, and though some do have a lot, they also pay huge fees for insurance in case sue-happy people attack them.

Where do you think corporations come up with the money to pay for insurance? It comes in the price of the goods sold. So when Micky D's raises the price of their burgers you know it's not just inflation, but more so, it's because of the continuous lawsuits and rising insurance costs. Who pays for these lawsuits or increased insurance costs? We do.

I'm starting to believe that the animal kingdom is much more in present time than the human race. Imagine a monkey sitting in a tree while eating his banana. When he's done, he accidentally drops it to the ground far below. At that very moment another monkey who is walking toward the most beautiful female monkey he's ever seen, slips and falls on that banana peel.

The female monkey points and laugh and walks away as the monkey on the ground sees where the banana peel came from. Quickly thinking, the monkey on the ground doesn't grab his back and start screeching in pain. On no, not this monkey. This monkey grabs that banana peel and heads up the tree to shove it up the other monkey's ass.

In the animal kingdom things get handled immediately. There is no long, drawn-out process, no hurt feelings that money can replace, and within a very short time frame, all is forgotten and one monkey is digging a peel out of his ass while the other is hitting up on the next strange monkey chick that comes along. Case closed. Animals are smarter than we give them credit for.

Are there any places where the law is handled instantly? I've heard that in some Middle Eastern countries a criminal that gets caught will go to jail on day one, is in court on day two, and by day three, depending on the crime if convicted as guilty, the criminal is either missing a hand for stealing or dead.

People know when they've done wrong. We don't need attorneys to exploit the person with hurt feelings. That person will find ways to be hurt even without the incident they're claiming.

Maybe I should go live in the jungle like our early ancestors. I may get my ass kicked by some gorilla, but at least I'd know my place and if I did overstep my boundary it would be dealt with right then and there.

Speaking of crimes, I think our prison system is much too lenient and expensive for the taxpayer. I understand that there are some super tough prisons out there, places like: Marion, IL; Maricopa County, AZ; Terra Haute, IN; and McCalister, OK. But there sure are a lot of light- and medium-lever prisons too. Not every prison should be like the Alcatraz of yesteryear, but I do believe that they should be overcrowded. Showers and haircuts should come once every six months and no more of this "three meals a day" crap. Each prisoner would have a little food stem to suck from like a rat in a cage. Their cell could have a little toilet, as most do, and the temperature would be kept at a level that made clothing unnecessary, no laundry.

Frankly, the jail cells should look like my first apartments. When I was starting out I didn't get three free meals a day, someone to do my laundry, or time to work out, read, and pick up a new language here and there.

Beds would be as simple as a rectangle shape of heavy cloth on the ground. No comfort for the prisoners. Maybe I could donate my old sofa bed that I used for ten years. It wasn't clean and definitely not comfortable.

Right now as it stands, prisoners get to work out, hang in the yard with their friends, read books, play video games, and get an education. I kind of hate that they get to educate themselves since they only seem to use it for all the wrong things…as if they're the victim. They study the law so they can use it to their advantage when they go for a court hearing. Break the law in order to get free food, free housing and increase your intelligence. What a deal!

As it stands, prisons are way too comfortable for the repeat offender. Oftentimes a criminal finds that he can't make it on the outside, so with prison they at least have shelter, food, clothing, and camaraderie. Prison should be hard, harder, the hardest. The inmates should spend most of their days and nights doing work and chores that support the outside world. We are paying for their food and shelter, we deserve something in return.

Think of all the money saved on the daily things criminals are being supported by. They have more luxury than people who are working hard to make ends meet. Hmmm, maybe I'll stop paying my taxes so I can go to jail and relax a bit. Yeah! That'll work!

The Mafia and Capitalism

First off, I'm not trying to get myself whacked, but by talking about the mafia, I should point out that I don't own a horse, but if I should wind up in bed with shrubbery from my front yard, I'll get the hint and shut my pie hole.

There are a lot of actual things to recognize about the mafia. They're not all a good guys and they're not all bad. Basically they're not as talked about as, but equally in line with, true capitalism. Let's think about this for a moment and compare the two: the mafia and the corporate world.

The reason the mafia has been around forever is because they actually have a good business model, aside from the killing stuff that is.

Like an entrepreneur, a guy starts out with some street smarts and some, maybe not so much, of the book smarts. Usually he has no inherited wealth, but if he has big dreams and big aspirations, wants to make some cash and climb his way to the top, he'll become crafty and sophisticated when the need arises. Strategically, he implements processes and through hard work and perhaps some violence, he'll fight tooth and claw to climb his proverbial career ladder. If he does outwork and out-strategize everyone and becomes stronger than his competition by hiring better help, he'll rise to the top, but not without really fierce competition. Instead of calling his business a corporation, he'll call it a family. And, like family, they all have worked together to make it through.

You might say that the American dream doesn't involve corruption, but I would probably respond with something like, "Do you know what the CIA does?" "Do you know why and how we're able to live the American dream?" Because of corruption at whatever level that suits the need.

Just like corporate America, once you're at the top everyone wants to bring you down, everyone wants your spot and the only way to keep your spot is if you stay sharp, keep your business model changing in order to keep up, or set the trends for the competition. You can't just sit there and count your money. If you do, you'll get taken over—just like capitalism. You've got a business and you've got to stay nimble. It's up to you in the mob to work your way up and to keep your spot. Nothing is ever inherited in the mob without a price.

Nothing is ever inherited without a price…that's a good point. Sure a mob boss's son might take over the family business, but it's not done without worthy experience to back it up. In corporate America sonny takes over daddy's seat and can easily ruin the company in a short order of time. Then people in the company start to leave or lose their jobs. In the mob, people who do what they're supposed to are well taken care of.

Whatever you, the reader, think at this moment, please don't believe I'm condoning that one goes out and becomes a member of the mafia, or tries to start a "family." I'm just doing a comparison of what works in this country and what doesn't. I'm contrasting the likeness of the mafia and corporate America. It's up to you to come to your own conclusions about which one treats their people better. Wink! Wink!

There is a major difference in the process of letting someone leave after being gainfully employed by either of the groups. In corporate America you might have a job that earns you a couple hundred thousand per year and then they pull a Donald Trump on your ass and say, "You're fired!" Then, you have to humiliate yourself and collect unemployment or try to explain in your future interviews why your services were no longer needed at your previous place of employment. Why, if you were so good at your job, they could stand to let you go.

With the mob, when you're fired...well, look on the bright side—no unemployment lines, no embarrassing interview questions and no worries whatsoever, cause you're really fired. But wait! There's more! Luckily, if you were a "family" member, and they take you out for a no-return lunch, if the firing was because of something major, they will usually compensate your spouse and child...kind of like an "in-house" life insurance policy. Smile and just think of the great shape you're going to be in after digging that hole in the ground. Okay, maybe a little morbid, but what the hell , it's my book.

Aside from the corporate comparisons, there is another aspect I appreciate about the mafia compared to other gangs in the world. When the mob decides to do a hit, they usually take out the immediate person/s necessary. It's in a professional, nothing personal, businesslike manner and the person knows exactly what they've done and usually other people (bystanders) don't get hurt. Whereas, these other gangs drive by a house and shoot out windows because there may or may not be someone in there that they want to kill, but instead, it's usually winds up as some little eight-year-old kid who was innocently watching cartoons. That's despicable! That's chickenshit!

Again, I'm not condoning everything the mafia does. I just recognize that they have certain ways of handling things that are so far off from how things are handled in by corporate America that it almost makes one wish there was a recruitment center for the mob. What is it, you might ask? It's like this: if a mob boss sees someone in their rank and file that is at the lower end, but is really productive, they don't care about the college education background, they bring that productive guy up the ranks as quickly as possible. In corporate America, you have to fight the good ol' boy routine or wait for your boss's nephew to screw up royally. Even still, when the nephew is gone, it doesn't mean you get the shot to prove your worth.

• • •

There is a story about a drug lord in a small town in Mexico along the Sierra Madre Mountains. It used to be quite the tourist attraction, but occasionally some of the tourist would wander out of town and a drunken Mexican would end up using them for target practice and kill them.

Well, word got out to the drug lord and he let it be known that if any tourist were killed that the person doing the killing would be tortured again and again before being killed themselves. Like the mob, the drug lord was taking care of his town's people. Tourists create income which enabled the small town to thrive while all others were failing. Though you may not agree with the drug lord and what he does for a living, you must understand that he does what he does because that's what he knows…kind of like a politician. It's all capitalism at its best and worst. You don't have to like it, but you'll always be living in it, whether you understand it or not.

Could you imagine if the mafia was run by democrats? Everyone would get the same percentage of the profit no matter how hard you worked or how many people you killed. Everyone would get the exact same waste management routes, taxation within the group would be the same as it is now, the guy at the top would tax himself the most. Can you imagine if it were a democratic mafia what the lawsuits within would be like? "Hey listen, you've got a better waste management route than me so I'm going to sue you. Matter of fact I'm feeling discriminated against because I'm not Italian enough." This shit doesn't happen because it's a well-oiled machine that runs congruent to its purpose. There's no penalty for doing well in the mob. Hmm, maybe crime does pay!

Like corporate America, the mob starts other legitimate businesses that employ people with real jobs, and through these subsidiaries, some money gets washed, which is another way of finding the tax loopholes that corporate America takes advantage of.

It sometimes seems that the mob is more in the real world than the socialistic society we're moving toward. I really don't recall the last time the mob started a war with another country based on "intelligence" from their field reps, such as the CIA.

If you were to remove the violence, the capitalistic or entrepreneurial aspects, the two groups are the same. To be truthful, I'm not so sure that there isn't a very quiet, yet subtle, under-the-radar approach to corporate violence. It just remains to be witnessed or revealed more effectively. Maybe one could conceive of the subtle corporate evils as the chemicals they put in your food or vices: sodas, cigarettes. There may not be bloodshed by weapons, but there is definitely death involved.

Now to contrast corporate America, the mafia, and the government, I appreciate the first two and loath the last. Sure, corporate America looks after their top-notch people, as does the mafia, as they should. The government, on the other hand, works at punishing the groups or individuals that perform well and create the huge amount of dollars the government needs...you want to talk about a bully in the room. The government takes from everyone who is earning their way in life and gives it to people who don't want to get off their fat ass to do anything constructive for themselves. It's totally backwards and corporate America and the mafia see this so they must take other actions to survive for the betterment of the group, the country.

It's all a ruthless game of victory from behind the veil. In our country everyone is punished by how well they do. The better the production the stronger the punishment... how jacked up is that?

Immigration Is Not for Illegal Aliens

O kay, I need to stress this point...I am going to talk about illegal aliens. Again, "illegal" aliens...I stress the word *illegal*. Don't you think it's important to enforce our borders? You have locks on your doors at home, right?

I want to be the first to offer a great new plan to our illegal alien problem, but first, I want to recognize those immigrants who have come to this country the right way. They took the proper "legal" steps to become upstanding citizens of our great country. The more the merrier, it's okay with me, come on in, but do it the right way. Our country has been built by people moving here from all walks of life, all countries. I love that cities like New York, San Francisco or Chicago have Little Italy, Greektown, and Chinatown. If we're going to be known as the "melting pot" then we need to have many different ethnic societies involved. These groups are what makes this country so great. The only thing that Americans are asking is that people who want to immigrate to the US, do it honestly, through the system.

Someone made a movie titled *A Day without a Mexican*, and tried to prove a point as to how valuable the culture is to our society. I agree wholeheartedly, they're very valuable.

Though they have their worth to society, it doesn't change the fact that many Mexicans are here illegally. They use our resources, take our jobs, don't pay taxes, and rarely, if ever, truly contribute to our system in a tax contribution sort of way. Guess who has to make up for the lack of lost tax revenue—those of us who are doing things legally.

I shouldn't just be using Mexicans as the source of our alien problem since there are many other cultures here as well. I do use the Mexicans because they are here from sneaking across the border that directly separates our country from theirs. The immigrants that made it here by using a temporary travel visa and then not going home at the proper time allotment, well, I'll deal with you later.

I thought of a few solutions that are on the true brink of ridiculous and I had a good laugh while doing so. For instance, what if everyone that was allowed to live in this country had a choker around their neck or something they carried on them that allowed them to pass through certain electronic checkpoints without getting blown to pieces? Then I figured, okay, that's kind of dumb because if I forget my choker one day, I might die…not a good thing!

As I thought more about it, I realized that everything in this country is based on the almighty dollar. Money is the reason for the illegal aliens in the first place. They come here to work and make enough money to send home, in turn creating a lifestyle that affords them some luxuries in their homeland upon their return. Some also come here to the US in order to support their families back home.

I feel for these people in the respect that they do what they can and take risks to help family survive, but at the same time, there has to be something they can do back home to guarantee their livelihood. There just needs to be more thought to their process.

Okay, so, everything is about the money! Well, let's set a law that states that any business that hires an illegal alien to work for them will be fined $100K for the first offense and $250k for the second. Also, these fines are like government-backed college loans…not excusable!

A corporation could not declare that, unbeknownst to them, one of their managers hired an illegal. It doesn't matter…get caught with an illegal alien working for you and you pay the fine.

How quickly would the illegal alien problem be resolved? If a contractor stopped by the nearest paint supply place to pick up a day laborer and the worker couldn't truly prove that he was here legally, but through broken English he told the contractor that he was, well, regardless of what the contractor is told, if it turns out the laborer is here illegally then the fine goes to the contractor.

"That's just not fair!" one might cry out. Yeah well, it seems there's a lot out there that just isn't fair…pay your fine!

Some might ask where the contractor is going to come up with $100K. That's not my problem. They wouldn't have to come up with it if they had just followed the rules. Everyone knows that you're not allowed to hire illegal aliens.

Now, don't ever let it be said that I'm not sympathetic toward someone's plight. I truly feel it's jacked up to have to pay these fines. If the government wasn't taxing us out the ass at every turn, then perhaps the contractor could afford to pay the $15 to $20 per hour for a legitimate employee instead of the $10 under the table.

Just think, how many individuals the government is screwing out of work right this minute. To have to pay a tax on a worker is the most ridiculous idea to date. An employer has to pay the government so he can hire someone that wants to make money so they can feed their family. This is so F'd up it clearly justifies the contractor's need to use the illegal aliens.

The government needs to step back and stop meddling in the free market economy. Yes, they should still be able to fine companies for using illegal aliens, but only after you've removed the "fines" (sometimes known as an employee tax) for hiring people in the first place.

How did the leaders of this country ever get so diluted in their thinking? Again, our founding fathers would be rolling over in their graves. This is not what they wanted. We were to have a free society that could earn a decent living. Now it's become a way for the government and its politicians to control and trivialize what means the most in America…FREEDOM!

Back to the lecture at hand…I don't mind immigrants who want to better their lives by leaving a country that won't grow. I understand why they want to come to America where they have a better chance of a better life. Just please, do it legally! I respect it! I encourage it! Just be a part of our beautiful country the right way, legally.

By legal I mean fill out the forms, wait the time period, and do what is expected and required so when the time comes, you don't have to always be looking over your shoulder for the INS. While you're waiting for the legitimate passports and green cards, read some books…learn the language and understand where it is you're coming to.

If America is such a great place to be then you should be more than willing to put some time and effort into becoming a legal citizen. It just makes sense.

America does offer the dream of a better life, but please don't come here on a six-month or education visa and expect that you can just stay because there are too many illegal aliens already and they'll never be able to find you.

Here is what I propose we do so when we implement the $100K fine so the company managers have a way to protect themselves ahead of time.

We can have an Internet Based Social Services Department (IBSSD) that a business's HR person can log into. When the HR person logs in, they can then enter a potential employee's social security number. Instantly, they will know if this applicant is hirable. If the SSN has been or is in use at multiple job locations that are an eye-opening distance away (perhaps separate states) then the HR person is required to delay that illegal alien through specified "hiring" tactics while the police or INS is contacted. If they don't make the report right away so the illegal alien can be caught, then they're fined. The log-in to the IBSSD and the call to the police can be confirmed for the business's cooperation.

"So now we're all responsible for turning in illegal aliens?"

In short, YES! Just like most topics I've discussed in this book, take the emotions out of it and look at the facts, look at the common sense.

Through the use of computers and the speed with which information is available these days, it wouldn't take long to know whether an employer was about to get himself in hot water with a fine that would bury his lifestyle completely.

Could you imagine that with every raid the INS does on a factory, if they caught just ten illegal aliens, that'd be $1 million. California might one day have a surplus of funds instead of being in tremendous debt. It really wouldn't take businesses very long to do the math and say, "Screw it! We're not hiring anymore illegal aliens."

Give grandma a job! All those sewing factories that are paying super-low wages right now, they do it, partially because they too are taxed out the ass by Uncle Sam. Again, remove the state employee tax so that companies can hire and pay a decent wage.

I know a lot of older people who would still work to make a few bucks in order to supplement the meager retirement check.

Are we too soft on illegal aliens? Are we bunching them in with the legal immigrants who did things the proper way? I personally think we are confused about who is who. We're okay with any culture being here, after all, this is America…the melting pot of the world, but when it comes to legal vs. illegal, I say Americans have their thoughts confused.

There is an area close to San Diego, California, where there are groups fighting for the illegal immigrants. Apparently there is a water canal/aqueduct that leads into this country, but the flow of the water makes it very dangerous and many illegal immigrants who try to swim their way into this country end up drowning. Signs have been posted in an effort to sway the immigrants from certain death. Now these groups are suing the state to have ropes and ladders placed in areas that will give the illegal immigrants a chance and not drown.

Now, I don't want anyone to die over the chance to live in this country, but I certainly understand not giving them a helping hand. I mean really, the next thing you know, these groups will be suing to make sure every prison gives the inmates a chance to escape. No guards with guns, no barbed wire and instead of giving them ladders to help with the escape, why don't we just take down the fences and give them all a shiny new Cadillac to drive away in.

We have immigration policies for a reason and the federal government needs to step up the work on tracking the illegal immigrants down and shipping them back to their homeland. Instead, we have a federal government that sues Arizona for trying to squash the immigration problem they're facing.

Through knowing that we have a great country with a great lifestyle to boot, we sometimes feel sorry for the immigrants in general and lump them together with the law-evading illegal aliens. Of course, everyone should get to experience America. That's what all immigrants want...a better life, and they can have it if they play the game correctly, they just need to do the proper work to become citizens. If they educate themselves, get jobs, and pay taxes, then they can send as much of their after-tax money to family back home, I don't really care.

They can open a business and make a gazillion dollars, as long as they do it legally. I would also hold them to the same scrutinizing rules as the rest of corporate America...

you hire one person who does not have the proper paperwork or is in this country illegally, you too pay the fines. This also means that you can't hire family members who are waiting on their immigration paperwork to return from our government. You can support them until they're legal, but they can't work or you get the fine.

Cities will go to endless means and spend countless dollars using traffic cameras to catch me driving 5 mph over the speed limit, but they won't go to the local Lowe's or Home Depot to stop the hiring of illegal laborers that are taking hundreds of thousands of dollars, if not millions, out of the job market for Americans...on a daily basis.

You can't tell me that Americans don't want these jobs. Trust me when I say, "They do." There are some contractors who are still working, building or painting homes. There are many out-of-work carpenters that need to feed their family and will take a lower wage if they must. To have to be in competition with an illegal alien is a disservice to the country and its people.

At the same time, I would tell all of these unemployed construction workers to get out of bed and get to the local hardware store so you can be hired instead of an illegal.

I almost forgot one thing about illegal aliens that I'd want to change. If someone is here in the US illegally and they have a baby, that child is not an automatic citizen of this country. First they are a citizen of their illegal parents' country. They can be considered to hold a secondary citizenship of the US, but it is limited. When the child is eighteen they will have the right to take the test and become a naturalized citizen. At any point before, if the parent is caught as an illegal, they will have to take the child with them to be exported.

This may seem a bit harsh, but really, how many illegal alien women come over and will get pregnant just to be able to stay in this country with their infant child who, by default, becomes a citizen? Quite a few I'm sure!

Tipping Isn't Just About Cows

I've got a tip for you: "Don't eat yellow snow!"

Ever wonder what really happened to the service industry? You know, when people really cared about their work regardless of whether they were going to receive a gratuity.

It appears that you can't do anything in America these days without someone putting their hand outward in anticipation of the tip. I don't mind, by the way, if they earned it...I just feel like people want tips just for showing up. Sound familiar?

Do you even know what tip stands for? It's an acronym: To Insure Promptness. Now, I appreciate it when someone is prompt with my order, but please, get the order right, care about my experience at the restaurant, don't act or feel like I'm inconveniencing you. You're the waiter, you took my order, if you know I asked for two eggs over-easy and one of the yolks is busted or overcooked, don't set that dish in front of me. Take it back to the cook and ask him to get the order right. Don't just expect me to accept it.

I don't care if you come to me and say, "Mr. Mancino, your food was ready but while I was bringing it to the table I realized that it just didn't measure up so I took it back to the chef and asked him to make a better presentation. It'll be just another minute."

If a waiter did this for me they'd forever be on my best friends list. I'd tell everyone I knew that if they're going to eat at that restaurant, they should request this waiter because they really care about the customer.

As it happens, I rarely get this kind of service and it bothers me. If I take a shirt into the cleaners and ask them to sew on a new button, more than half the time I get the shirt back without a new button. I took a pair of pants to the tailor so he could take in the waist. When I got the pants back everything looked good, but evidently, as I would come to find, nothing was good. I flew out of town on a business trip and when I dressed for the day I found that my pants still had the same waist, but the legs were about four inches shorter. It was supposed to be a quick trip so I hadn't packed a second pair. Needles to say, I felt out of sorts and this came through in my performance as I didn't close a bunch of deals that day. I dress for success and if you do the same, you know what I mean.

Is it that difficult to pay attention to your job and make sure you're doing things right? I ask for no mustard or pickles on my burger so what happens? I get extra mustard and pickles. I ask for my luggage to show up on time in the right city and it ends up in New Jersey. My favorite is when one of my pieces of luggage makes my flight yet the rest of it ends up on a different plane. I picture the luggage guy shooting the shit with his coworker and just randomly whipping luggage onto different conveyor belts. "Hey John, toss this one on the belt to Albuquerque and the one next to it to Dallas. Where we going to lunch today?" It should be a crime that my luggage has been on better trips than me.

Maybe it's just me and my stroke of finding service people that don't care, but really, I can't be that unlucky that often. My guesstimation is that the reason it happens so often is because people just don't care enough about their job or their career anymore. Again, they're just going through the motions.

With this continuous experience of shoddy or half-assed service I began wondering what could be done to improve society's service standards. Commissions?

What if everyone had to work on commission? It would solve a lot of issues rather quickly.

With each bill you got at your favorite eatery there could be a questionnaire to be filled out. Was your server: A) Pleasant, B) Incredibly Nice, C) Disappointing, D) What server? Wouldn't it be great if the tip was based on this? What if the waiter had to sit there and take the feedback from the customer? Wouldn't that be great?

Why is 20 percent acceptable? How are you shortchanging yourself by thinking that you'll automatically get 20 percent? Who is sitting at your table? Who is coming through your business door? Please, for God's sake, make me want to be in your shop, store, or diner. Make me want to come back. Make me want to tell all of my friends about your place. Make me want to give you 30 percent!

Anytime a server engages me in quick and simple conversation that acknowledges my existence, other than the fact that I'm sitting in their section, and if they get my order right, they're going to receive the token of my appreciation in a higher than normal tip. I'm not looking for the guy that says, "Hey, I'm a vegetarian and though I work at this steakhouse, I don't really know which cut of steak to recommend." Set your personal views or history aside and serve me.

With my commission idea, after I'm done eating, depending on the service and frequency of my server, I'd get my bill and also get to rate the server. Then, at the end of each week or month, the owner of the establishment would be able to see which of the servers is really making a difference for the customer. If the server was highly rated by the customers, there would be a commission or percentage of sales kicked back to that server.

The questionnaires could even ask other pertinent information: How was your dish presented? Was your food served hot, warm, or cold? Did your server have good communication skills? Was your seating area clean?

I sometimes think that everyone in the world should be on some type of commission system. Could you imagine what would happen if police officers had to change the way they handle a speeding driver? Perhaps their ratings across America wouldn't be so bad. It seems that over the years cops have become known more as bullies than someone you're happy to see. We constantly see reports in the news about racial profiling, or officers being too quick on the draw, oftentimes pulling people over for absolutely no real reason, but using a cracked tail-light as an excuse. What if we could get America to love cops the way they love firemen? Maybe they could enforce the rules, but be nicer about it. Maybe smile from time to time.

So, how would a commission work on an officer of the law? That's easy. After you get done signing for the ticket, you'll receive a bail notice in the mail a week or so later. With this bail amount, there again, could be a questionnaire: Did the officer treat you respectably? Did he advise you of your options?

Of course, this questionnaire would have to be filled out when you're not so upset about having received a ticket in the first place. Truth be known, you know if you really deserved the ticket, you know when you've done wrong. It may be a pain in the ass and costly to get caught at something, but in reality, it only happened because you weren't following rules that were put in place for everyone's safety. Now answer the questionnaire.

Have you ever been on the phone with a 1-800 call center and you can tell the operator on the other end just doesn't want to be there? It happens all the time. Sure, they may not have the most exciting job in the world, but really, can they at least talk or pretend like they care? There have been times where I can hear the apathy in their voice and I decide to change their outlook on things. I'll often ask the person where they're located? How is the weather there (since it's usually far from where I am)? I do anything I can to make that person know that I care. Perhaps if they did the same thing, they'd like their job better. I can't think of anything more appreciated than someone being of great service to another.

Think of all the jobs out there that could be performed better if there was a commission. I don't believe you should do your job enthusiastically based solely on the idea you're going to get more money just because you put a smile on your yap, I'd prefer you just be great at it, but if a commission helps, so be it. Money is not the end-all or be-all, but it helps. Doctors, dentists, engineers, teachers, construction workers, pilots, mechanics, barbers, cashiers, nurses, plumbers…you name it, the world would get better if there was a commission involved.

Let me share an experience with you regarding service and tipping. Well, ever since I can remember, I've been regularly using the bathroom on my own. I learned to wash my hands before and after the act. Before, because I don't know what I may have touched throughout the day, and after, because it just makes sense.

So here I am, visiting a fine restaurant. Because I sometimes have the bladder of a seven-year-old or a pregnant lady, I must use the restroom more often than others. Upon entering, I notice a man sitting next to the towel dispenser. While I'm taking care of business the guy might shoot the shit with me (no pun intended) about the latest sports or something a little less trivial. When I finish my business and wash my hands he is there to hand me a paper towel. Looking at a small basket that's been appropriately set on the counter, it's full of one-dollar bills…tips for handing out paper towels. What a load of (Place expletive here)! I get the idea of paying for a spritz of cologne, or throwing in a buck for some breath mints so you don't knock out your date, but really, pay for a paper towel?

Let me share with you how I think it should be done. There is a place I frequent in New York and the bathroom attendant actually deserves and earns a tip. He keeps the bathroom really clean, he has jazz music or the local game playing, there's a variety of mints, gum, and even some colognes. While squirting some soap into your hand or turning on the water he'll offer some small talk. When all is done, he actually hands you a real towel. This guy makes people feel special, even in a bathroom. He works for it. He doesn't just put a seat in the bathroom and hand you a paper towel in exchange for money, those type of guys aren't doing shit!

Tip...To Insure Promptness! The guy hasn't insured anything that I couldn't insure on my own. Where is he when I need to stop at McDonald's and take care of business? There seems to be a guilt trip going on in the men's restrooms across America.

One time I decided to do a little survey. I'd occasionally stand back and watch to see if everyone tipped this guy who sat around handing out paper towels all day. As it appeared, many guys don't wash their hands when the steward is there. In my survey I found that many men don't carry cash on them and others just felt so guilty about having to pay the guy that they'd rather avoid eye contact and walk out without washing their hands. Now this bathroom guy has become a barrier to clean hands. Ironic, isn't it?

Is this steward doing a disservice to the country? I may visit the restroom three or four times in a couple of hours and be out a few bucks. I'm seriously thinking about shitting all over myself and then pay him to clean me up. Earn that dollar, damn it!

•   •   •

If it's not about tipping then it's about human kindness. Just once I'd like to go to the airport in Los Angeles or New York and not be under suspicion. It'd be nice to have people respond to the simple word of "hello." Imagine if these people were on commission, how great the process at the airport would be. How great would all the places one travels to throughout the week, month, or year be if the employees were competing for your approval.

I travel all over the country and I come across some security people (metal detector people) that are awesome. I noticed that in airports like Scottsdale, AZ, and Ft. Meyers, FL, there are some retiree types that seem to be on their second career. Maybe it's the way the older folks were brought up, but they just seem to treat you so much better. With a smile they'll ask how you're doing, yet they remain very professional at their post. I believe that they probably realize most people are just trying to make their way through and that the majority are not terrorists. Then again, perhaps it's because these older folks come from an era that truly cared. They're just used to treating people with respect. They're detailed in regards to security and searches, but a lot nicer about it.

Let me ask you this, "If your salary was $20K but you knew you could make $50K just by being nice...how quick would you change?" If you answered, "Real quick," then you're the one this book is for. You need to find a place within yourself that gives regardless of your salary. No one made you take that job for whatever the pay is, you agreed to it.

I'm not sorry that I'm reiterating the fact that I'm truly amazed when people make the same amount of money as their coworker whether they're nice or mean. I guess it really is a cruel world. In my world, everyone would work on commission. The ones that are good at their jobs make more than the ones that are crap...end of story! No excuses!

Of course this is hypothetical, but the fun in this book is that people can learn to think differently. Just think differently... What if?

It Shouldn't Be That Easy!

I don't want to pick on cops like they're criminals, because they do see the worst of the worst on a daily basis and I really do appreciate everything they do for us. I just believe that it shouldn't be so easy to become a police officer, a fireman, or a teacher. As a matter of fact, any job that requires one to work with the public in a tougher-than-normal way, I think needs to be backed up by much more education. Hear me out and don't judge me yet... the jobs of policemen and teachers are some of the most important roles we have in society. Many are great friends of mine, but I still see a huge demand for these jobs with short supply of great candidates. In other words, I want these jobs to be the most desirable jobs out there. We need the best talent fighting for these jobs.

There are some officers who were bouncers at a bar somewhere and hit the ripe old age of twenty-six before they noticed that all their buddies were in careers.

Many of these guys, with only a high school education, see the dollar signs and the fact that they can have benefits, pensions, respect, and so many other things: they figure that it's the best road to take. They don't have a passion for it like some people who dreamed of it since childhood.

I want to see the person who has dreamed of being a cop his whole life achieve that goal. He's educated himself to get a criminal justice degree and he wants the job because it has a huge pay scale upside. Again, let's pay these people more so we get the right people breaking down the doors to get the job.

Becoming a police officer should take a four-year criminal justice degree with backgrounds in psychology and a program that teaches them how to deal with the crap from the get-go. But no, they go through a few months of physical and memory training to come out with a weapon and a career.

They should have to go through an array of classes that deal with real-life situations and not get it from a textbook or an academy-trained instructor. Big jobs take big training. Take a look at doctors; they go through years of training and education. I think it should be similar for teachers and police officers.

I know someone isn't going to like this, but so what. There are too many immature officers with huge egos that get caught up in the moment and can't control themselves. If you've ever talked to a retired cop and they tell you any of the stories, the things they've lived through, you can hear in their voice how caught up they were and at times you can even hear the regret of not still being in the mix. This job is super hard and super taxing on your body, brain, and family. We need to reward these people with better, higher pay. It's not an easy job, so it shouldn't be so easy to get.

As for firemen, I'm glad they're there when you need them, the same way I am when I need the police. My little pet peeve with firemen is this ten days on and twenty days off per month.

If you Google "Why become a fireman?" you'll see information like: 98 percent of firemen are never laid off. The job is theirs for a lifetime. This includes pension plans, medical benefits, and the most flexible schedule I've ever seen. It offers the ability to have a second job, to be a local hero, and by all measures, to be in what seems like a college fraternity.

At times, firemen have light enough duty as it is. When they're not attending to a fire or auto accident, they're cruising the business sections or apartment buildings for code violations. I'm not sure that requires ten days on and twenty days off per month. I understand that there are going to be some really bad days of work, but if it's so bad, how can there be enough resourceful energy to have a second job or business.

Sorry guys, just my opinion. Again, many of these guys have side jobs. How do you have time for a side job? Let's pay them more and jam more tasks into their week. This job is already desirable just based on the amount of days they work per month. It should be harder to become a firefighter. Let's give them great money instead of just good money and no room in their day for a side business.

I would give them the time off if their every waking hour at work was like it is when they have to do a wilderness fire or fight a blaze that covers half of southern California. Kudos to those men and women, they need the time off. I just wish my company would adopt this policy, whereas, when I work twenty hours a day for three days in a row, then I get three off.

Let's cut to the chase here. Another job that people should really have more of an education for is teaching. Again, go and Google "Reasons to become a teacher." You'll see things like: never get fired, get three months off for summer. Everyone knows a teacher somewhere that skated through the easy college work to get their credentials so they could get off work by 3:30 and have the summers off.

If you knew how many people in college told me that they wanted to become teachers just so they could have the summers off, you'd flip! Their thoughts were that it is an easy major, great hours, and whole summers off. That's appalling! I want the best and brightest to have the desire to be teachers because they really love kids and want to help develop young minds, and then make some serious cash.

This is not to belittle the great teachers out there who chose their careers because of their passion for education. I have been lucky enough to have had some incredible teachers, as have my kids. With that being said, there are some out there in the school system that should not be teaching: you know who you are. Most of your students fail your class because you don't know how to communicate properly to individuals. You probably weren't that great in school while growing up, but now that you're in the system, you find it hard to leave.

The average teachers don't get fired or pushed out of the school system and that's a problem. Go check the stats on how many teachers are let go of their jobs due to bad performance. You'll be utterly shocked and then shocked some more.

I think the teachers need to be in competition with each other, just like the rest of the world. The last industry we need any entitlements in is education. This is the industry that is supposed to help build our future as a solid country. We cannot settle for mediocrity. Again, overpay the great ones like crazy and push the bad ones out. Do it for the kids, do it for our country. We need our kids to dominate the world in education.

Using math for our example, each kid should have to take a test at the beginning of a semester to determine exactly what that student understands. Then at the end of the semester, if that kid that usually carries a D average isn't up to a B or better, the teacher doesn't get her commission. Do you think that teacher would spend extra time with that student? Do you think that the teacher would get a bit more creative to get through to the child? I do! Money is a great incentive/driver. That's reality!

It'd be interesting to see how many ways a teacher could learn to communicate with individual students, on their level. Teachers don't need to focus on every student because there are some that will always get the A grade. What the teacher could or should do is to pair students up. Put an A student with a D or C student. Let them learn how to help their peers. Eventually they'll deal with them, whether it's today or tomorrow, they're going to deal with them. Kids, welcome to your society.

As a matter of fact, let's talk to the kids for a moment. Why do you let yourself fail or not try harder to be the best you can be? Don't tell me that you are trying and can't get past a C. That's BS. Are you in school for the fashion show or to get an education?

I know that there are a lot of students that do try and do bring their grades up. Kudos to you.

Back to the teachers. How often do you fold when a kid needs to pass a class or he won't be the star of the football team? How often do you call a kid to come back to your class after school so you can tutor them? If you know a kid is failing don't you see that as a reflection of your communication skills? Kids aren't stupid, they just may not understand exactly what you're saying.

There was once this little boy who couldn't understand his times tables. Tutor after tutor tried to teach this boy. Then one day a tutor came along and asked the kid what the x meant in the math problem. The kid couldn't answer because no one ever took the time to explain what it meant. He saw it as an x, not as the word "times" or "multiplied by." Problem solved.

How are you communicating? If you have a student that is failing, then you're failing. Step it up! These kids need you to be a professional and help them to understand.

If we put these teachers on commission I'm pretty sure the results would increase dramatically. I'm sick and tired of hearing that we don't have the best teachers because the pay is so low. Increase it then, but ask more from them. Limit the number that can become teachers and only take the cream of the crop. Wouldn't it be awesome if a lot of those kids that are furthering their education to become lawyers, architects, and engineers put their mind toward teaching because it paid as much as those other occupations? Young adults are getting over the idea that a job is glamorous and are more interested in what will pay well.

There is a school in a really rough area of Chicago that I think could be a role model for all schools around the country. This school pounds it into the students' heads that they will work their asses off while in school. The kids are taught that they will be great, they will be focused, they will be honest, they will be accountable, they will not be violent, they will believe in themselves and their peers, and they will absolutely go to college. I repeat, they will go to college—PERIOD!

The school proudly hangs acceptance letters all around the school. Guess what? All the seniors go to college. Let me remind you, this school is in a really tough and violent area of Chicago.

The school is run with very challenging rules which are strictly adhered to by the faculty and the students. The school days are longer than the average school and the dress code is a formal uniform. The parents are required to be involved and not just be helicopter parents, there to baby their child. The school is run like a professional business and it works very well.

Imagine if our whole education system was run like this, we'd be a powerhouse. Think about the number of awesome young adults we would be pumping into society. Imagine if the government was run like this…we'll talk about that later.

Parenting: What Were You Expecting?

Listen! We all have our challenges at home and no family life is perfect, however, I've noticed that things have shifted on the home front for many. Back in the day it was an honor to have the ability to have one parent stay at home with the kids. It was a sign that things were going well for the family and the parent at home was fortunate enough to have significant influence over the growth of the children. Well, these days the shift has turned into a complaint about how hard it is to be at home with the kids. Like always, I'm shocked!

Why do stay at home parents complain about being home and raising children? Do people feel like they're missing something at work? Do you think that people at work are missing things at home? I know that I would much rather have seen my child's first tooth fall out rather than meet my first client in the worst part of town in a heavy rainstorm. When I'm on my deathbed I won't be thinking about those audit meetings I thoroughly enjoyed. I'll be thinking about those days at home with the family.

Oftentimes, my buddies share with me about their marital dilemmas. Though they don't go into extreme depth, the message conveyed is that they feel somewhat victimized by the very person that is supposed to be supporting them mentally. I understand that everyone has something going on at home that can be considered a dilemma or out of whack. What I don't understand is when a husband has to be on the defense regarding his work or the fact that he's not the stay-at-home parent. Sometimes I feel sorry for these guys who have to apologize for working late or not being home early. In my house, which isn't perfect by any stretch of the imagination, we use a lot of common sense. In other words, we both understand the importance of the different roles in the family. These roles, which we adhere to, is the fuel that makes the engine run smoothly.

Both my wife and I have very specific and important roles in the family. I take care of my role to earn some money in order to pay the bills while my wife's role is to be home during the day and raise our children. Let me be clear: both are functions of each other, but raising children is the most important role in the world. Be proud of it!

Too many times I hear of women getting pissed off at their husbands for doing this or that, when in fact I know the husbands are working their collective asses off to support their families. It just pains me to see them lose their self-respect to their partner that stays home all day and thinks that managing a household is a tougher job than dealing with strangers while on the road or working in a factory or on a construction site to earn a living. I get that they are both challenging but one of them is much more rewarding and it's not the factory or construction site option.

Having kids isn't about having a cute handbag while running around town with a little Chihuahua and a baby.

It's about hard work and raising children. It isn't about tuning your kids out while scanning through the latest *US Weekly* or *People* magazine.

Managing a house is hectic, but not as awful as it's made out to be. Tough and awful is not a good way to describe being with your kids as you're coaching them through life.

I would much rather be at home with my kids all day than stuck in a cubicle or somewhere in a big office crunching numbers in the latest Excel spreadsheet. Does it really sound that great to commute an hour each way to do a job that sucks? Do you really think your husband enjoys talking to Frank in the mailroom more than hanging out with the kids? Unless, of course, Frank is super cool and makes him laugh his ass off, then that's another story...I'm kidding!

Seriously, people, what were you thinking? I'm talking to you, the women who work at home while your husbands leave for work all day. Remember, it is called "work." Then, he comes home to continue working. It's as though you believe that the job he was doing all day wasn't that hard, but you being at home was awful. So now, he needs to take over at home too. Are you going to stay up all night and finish the outstanding plumbing work, construction work or PowerPoint presentations that need to be done?

Ladies, you're not invisible! It's unfortunate that I can hear what is happening to men across the country. Though I do have to admit, some men let themselves be treated like crap and many are afraid to put their foot down, but still, where's the respect?

That's a great question, when did the respect get replaced? I'm not saying that we need to go back to the fifties where the men were greeted with slippers, the newspaper and a stiff drink when they got home from work, but would it be so difficult to let each other know that they're appreciated for their job and contribution to the family.

I am proud of the fact that that my wife and I are a team. In fact, she is my inspiration. She starts her day with respect for herself and our family, first by keeping her body and mind fit, but also, she comes home and makes sure everyone in the house is set for their day.

I travel a lot for work and my wife thoroughly understands that I do it for our family. I hate traveling. I hate airports, cabs, and hotels. The moment I enter a hotel room, I spend at least fifteen minutes disinfecting the door knobs, TV, remotes, and anything else I may lay my hands on. I'm rarely able to sleep in a hotel due to the bed bugs that I think are always crawling on my skin. I actually sleep in sweatpants, socks, and a long-sleeve shirt. If I could sleep in a mummy suit within airtight bubble, I would.

My wife knows I'd rather be at the park or shooting hoops with the kids. We have our priorities and that is family first. It's not her first, me first, or the kids first, it's family first. What I mean by that is, whatever the biggest need is, that will get the most attention. If I have a 6:00 a.m. flight, my wife has helped to make sure I've got what I need. She doesn't bitch and moan because I'm on the road again and she'll have to deal with the kids by herself; she completely understands this to be part and parcel of our teamwork as husband and wife.

While out on the road, going from town to town, I get in conversations with men all the time. In one instance

I was talking to a guy and I could tell he was a little bit down. As it turns out, he was trying to figure out how to tell his wife that he had to drive to some Midwestern city for business and he would have to leave that night. He just knew she was going to be pissed. Hearing this from him, I just had to say, "Dude! It's not like you're going to Vegas." He shook his head, and in my mind, I felt sorry for the guy. He was a broken man. Let me reiterate once again, this guy was afraid to tell his wife that he had to drive five hours to go handle his job, his work! The mortgage and meal ticket!

I've known this guy for a few years and he has a stay-at-home wife who doesn't do that much; she's not involved in her kid's school, no work, no housework—since she has a cleaning lady and the breakfast for the kids consists of cold Pop-tarts. He, on the other hand, gets up each day to go to work, often has to travel for work (not for play), comes home to help the kids with their homework, participates in the kid's sports when he can, and seems to be doing a hell of a lot more than her. Where's the balance?

I see a lot of guys doing this and I think it's great and important part of being a parent. I'm that guy who works a lot of hours and has a full-time job at home. I love it! That's living! My wife loves it! One day your kids will be grown and you won't be able to help them with homework or life's challenges. So take the time now to embrace it! Enjoy it! Stop complaining about it! Never complain about staying home with your kids like you were laying bricks in twenty-below-zero weather.

There are some things that just drive me crazy and when I hear about men losing their "manhood," because some woman thinks it's okay to berate him, sometimes as a daily regimen, I thank God I never have to fear losing my voice in our house and that I have a wife that is sensible and understands we are a team. I don't know that I could ask for more. Even the lottery wouldn't suffice to this.

Well, okay, maybe the $100,000,000 lotto wouldn't be all that bad.

So, how is this happening…men losing their ability to be men? Is it normal for a woman to be attracted to a man because of his earning power and then after years of marriage the woman slowly erodes every ounce of respect the man has? Is it that men really want to be subservient to a woman? Somehow, I don't think so. I've never heard a guy say, "You know, Vince, one day I want to get married so I can work my ass off all day and deal with a lot of angry people at my job. Then I want to come home to get beaten down by my spouse, wouldn't that just be the dream life?" Or, "Vinny, my man, I can't wait for the day where I work construction all day and come home to be told my day was easy compared to my wife's."

As I said, I've never heard a guy say anything near this, yet, that's what I hear is happening day after day across America.

Is it in the food? I hear that beef and chicken, the main courses for dinners across this country are filled with hormones…estrogen! I mean really, they say the hormones in milk and meat are doing things to the male body, giving men boobs, so is it possible the food has also weekend the man's mind? There has to be an answer somewhere. I'm not saying the choice of meat at your dinner table is the answer, but somehow or other, men are lacking the testosterone in their system that once made them MEN.

So when did it become okay for a stay-at-home mom/wife to bitch about her husband going to work? Perhaps the roles should be reversed for a day or two, or maybe a month. I know a great deal of men that'd love to stay home and not go to work, not deal with crazy people at their company and not have to look for ways to appease their spouse every time they had to do something that put a roof over their head, food in their stomach, clothes on their back, and an incredible lifestyle to one-up their neighbors and friends.

I'm just saying, there has to be a balance somewhere and if there isn't, something will give way, the dam will break. By the way, back to the kids... Ladies, do you think it's healthy for your kids to hear you complain about being home with them?

•   •   •

I know it seems like I'm bashing here, but maybe you're not hearing what I am saying. Maybe your man is too afraid of you to share his thoughts about anything? I find it interesting that a lot of women think men don't share their feelings or their emotions. Sometimes this thought makes me have to laugh. Men share plenty of feeling and emotions; they just no longer do it with the ones who are making them feel like crap. Men are actually reaching out to their brethren (if you will) and asking the infamous question, WHY ME?

It's kind of funny, but not "ha ha" funny, that guys will often share how their wives are pissed because all he wants to do at the end of the day is have some fun with the kids, do some homework, play catch in the yard , try to unwind, and not think about his day. Whereas, when he gets home, all his wife wants to do is unload about how her day was and how she had to shuffle the kids back and forth. I mean, really? Shuffle the kids here and there? What's so bad about that? Again, it may be hectic, but really, it's not as awful as it is made out to be.

Again, what were you thinking? You wanted kids. Did you not know kids need to be taken places and paid attention to? What did you think was going to happen? You were going to have kids and they'd develop by themselves? If I travel three or four days out of the week and I come home late on a Friday evening, I know I have to get up early Saturday morning to take the kids where they need to be. There's no guessing game about it. I wasn't thinking that having kids was going to be someone else's thing to deal with. I think anyone that uses their kids as a reason for how tough life is, either doesn't really like their kids or second, really can't stand themselves and their life.

I've said it before: If you complain about being with your kids then maybe you just don't like them and perhaps it's because they're just like you.

I actually thoroughly enjoy my kids' lives. I have a stressful job and I work my ass off so I can provide for my family, so we can share great experiences together. I never second-guess why I am where I am. I have a direction and a discipline that let me acknowledge I'm right where I want to be.

•   •   •

So, ladies, I have to ask: are you preparing your husband's life or his death? Does he look forward to coming home to you or does he look forward to an early grave? In the deep recesses of his mind, are you a comfort or drain on his respect and confidence?

How are you showing him that you appreciate what he's giving you? When was the last time you gave him a full-body massage? Yes, you heard me…a body massage! You know, just so you could help take the weight of the world off of his shoulders.

Are you creating intimate moments for you and your husband to be alone? You know, a nice dinner out in a secluded, romantic restaurant? Have you kept the spark in the bedroom alive? Has he been rejected by you so many times that he's given up trying? Now, I understand this can go both ways, but for a man, if he's sexually satisfied he doesn't usually have anything else in the world he'll feel he needs. There's nothing in the world he'll feel he can't conquer. Help to build him up and for you he'll handle anything the world throws at him.

As most adults know, the way to a man's heart is not always through his stomach. This thought might be a bit shallow, but often quite true.

If you ask your husband when he comes home in the evening, "How was your day?" and he doesn't really want to talk about it, just know that this might be his way of keeping you protected. He may want to leave the office where it is and just come home to someone who loves him and appreciates what he does for the family. No man ever had big dreams of being an accountant, plumber, or garbage-man, but they do what it takes to get by and take care of the family.

If a man isn't willing talk to with you, perhaps you've made him afraid to open up. The way women just want men to listen without always "fixing" the problem, is the way men want you to listen. When you do offer advice, like directions, a man most likely will find the way on his own.

•   •   •

The Cunningham's, from the *Happy Days* sitcom, I don't expect, but is there anything so wrong with being a little like Mrs. C? I mean, look at her. She was always impeccably dressed, offered good advice to Howard and always served up a good meal without a hair out of place. It doesn't hurt to be proud of your role.

"Well, Vincent, that's just a TV show."

Sure, it may be a TV show of the past, but there's no reason a woman can't get out of bed like they would for a job and get ready for the day. Be on top of your game by the time the kids wake up. Treat it like a job. Set a good example for your kids. If you struggle with mornings or are not a "morning person" then your kids will be the same exact way.

Set a new routine; get out of bed and make yourself up for the day, get a jump start and make sure the family is adjusted and prepared for the day ahead. If you had a job outside of the home would you sleep in, not shower, throw on some sweats, be late for work and meetings? Remember, you're not in college anymore. It's not cool to always be late and running behind schedule every morning. Your kids are the ones that will suffer.

One difference between my wife and some other stay-at-home moms is she's resilient with her time and discipline. At times, I think she cares more about our family than she does herself. Do I always share this thought with her? No, but I sincerely believe it to be true. Truth of the matter, I wouldn't want her to be any other way. She's got my back and I have hers. The way a marriage should be. She certainly believes her role is just as important as mine if not more. She treats her role just like a job outside the home. It is not, and never will be, a burden.

• • •

Somehow or other, women have flipped it on society and have made men in particular believe that what they do at home all day with the kids is hard work. I hear men declaring, almost parroting one another, "Boy, I wouldn't want to do what they do. It's a job staying home." How would a man know if it's hard to stay home and care for the child? Oftentimes, he only knows by what he is told. Even then, what's so "hard?" Wouldn't you rather do the job at home with your kids?

Is it a mental challenge? Yes! Is it challenging? Yes! Does it test our patience? Yes! Does it wear you out? Yes! Is it the greatest job in the world? Yes! Keep in mind that jobs outside the home are challenging, test your patience, and wear you out.

Let's look at this for a moment. Babies tend to sleep most of the day. When they are awake you give them attention. If they're crying, it's a form of communication.

Since they can't vocalize yet, they're letting you know they want something. If this gets you riled because you can't figure out what they need, that's on you, have patience. Normally, the baby is hungry for some milk/formula or may have a dirty diaper. There aren't usually a lot of things a baby will cry for, unless you change the channel on a good show, but hey, I'd cry too. By the way, they're only babies for so long. Soon, they'll be off to school for most of the day. I know that taking care of a baby is super demanding but it's for a short amout of time. Your husband has to be an electrician for 40 years!

As the baby gets older and perhaps is a year old or so, having them awake can be and is pleasurable. I think when parents get frustrated by being home with their child, it's because they aren't mentally stimulated by another adult. So what! Stimulate your mind by getting down to their level on the floor and sharing the experience of a toy your child is touching or inspecting for the first time. The wonder is in watching an infant observe and learn things that we take for granted. If you have a tough time and consider that to be work, well, I feel sorry for you. Remember, they'll be in high school before you know it, so take it in, embrace it, and find the joy it.

Anytime I hear a person bitch and moan, man or woman, about having to cart their kids off to here or there, I think about how selfish they are and they must not really be enjoying the experience anymore. If this is the case, then perhaps things should be switched up a bit. If you have teenagers, have you thought about getting involved in something with them? You might take a guitar class together, join a chess club, or learn to play golf with one another. What I really suggest is that you have some alone time with your kids.

If you have more than one kid and they have different tastes in hobbies, then split the time up so each child gets your undivided attention. I would also get rid of cell phone use during these excursions. When your kids are older, perhaps adults, wouldn't it be nice to know that you got to share some really great moments with them. Trust me, one day they'll tell their friends how great you are/were as a parent, all because of the time you spent with them.

Sometimes busy parents forget how important it is to have time with the kids. If you can remember how your toddler used to run up to you when you'd been gone for a while, well, whether they're kids are in their teens or not, believe me when I say that they still enjoy your company. Whether they'll let their friends in on their need for the connection with you, well…that's another story.

Just be glad for the time you have with them before they are embarrassed to be seen with you. Trust me, that day will come soon enough.

•   •   •

How is the household running? Not that everyone should have over-the-top standards, but then again, I know of some people who could raise their standards. Who runs the house, you or your kids? Is little Johnny's room a mess or does he have to keep it clean? I heard one excuse from a parent, "Well, it's his room. Everything in there is his and if company comes over we just close that door."

Wow! Did you know there was a time when kids had to make their bed before they left for school? Did you know there was a time when kids didn't get allowance for cleaning their bedrooms? Did you know that there was a time these simple disciplines made a child care about their environment? I ask again, who is running the household?

My kids get to enjoy sports, which we pay for. My kids get to have nice things, which we pay for. My kids get to go places and do things...wait for it...which we pay for! My kids don't get an allowance, but they do get to work for the nice things they want. This will not only build character, but also an appreciation for what they have.

There was this show on TV called *The Nanny*. A family is out of control, usually because the mom and dad couldn't agree on how to raise the kids or one was being too lenient. They had unruly children that had no respect for anyone: mom, dad, or siblings. Some of the kids had unkempt bedrooms with toys strewn all over. Why, because the home was out of balance. In most of these cases, the husband worked all day to come home to a mess. This shouldn't be happening. I suggest a dad should flat-out stop paying for anything until the kids pick up their crap. Again, a family is supposed to be a team.

By the end of one week with the Nanny, the kids were under control, the parents learned to work as a team, and the home life soon became balanced. It shouldn't take a stranger to help square your house away. It should only take some good ol' fashioned disciplining. I'm not talking about bringing out the belt as I don't believe in that form of punishment, but I do believe in solid communication. It may not work the first, second, or third time, but you have to keep trying to get through to your kids.

I guess I kind of prove my point I made earlier in the last chapter. This country is raising a bunch of spoiled children that don't care what anyone says. There are more social misfits than there ever was while I was growing up. You can't blame TV or YouTube for that.

If I were some of these parents that I'm speaking of, and you know if you fall into this category, I'd go home and write out everything I observed happening in my home. If the kid's room is a shambles, write down what you see. If you have dinner at the table as a family and the TV is on or the kids are texting, write it down. Don't take any actions until you have a clear understanding of what's happening in your household. Then…

The first person to deal with is your spouse. Go for a walk and talk. This is where you get out of the house and begin sharing everything you wrote about. The reason I don't suggest you do this in the house just yet is because when you're in public it's not likely you'll start arguing aloud. Besides, a walk is good for you and can help you breathe better when you're looking at turmoil.

Show your list to your spouse. Your home life should have beliefs, rules, goals, and principles. Make a pact to really work on everything, but not all at once. As I said, you truly have to understand what you're up against. If the home life is unbalanced it didn't just happen a day or two ago. Work on one thing at a time and my suggestion would be to work on your partnership first because you'll need the support of each other when you start putting order in on the kids.

How you handle your written observations is really your business and trying to handle it by shouting or not sticking to your demands becomes futile. If your kid is told that there won't be any texting at the dinner table, and it continues, turn the phone off for a month...but be strict about it.

To some, this might not seem to be reality, but yet it is. I see it day in and day out in the working world. Little kids have grown up spoiled (not always with wealth) but by lack of disciplining.

•   •   •

I'll tell you, I've met a lot of people who really have it good as stay-at-home parents, and I think some of them really take it for granted. I'll say it over and over...you get to spend a lot of time with your children, it's a blessing! Raise your hands and be proud of it!

I think there needs to be a TV show that instead of trading spouses, these very fortunate stay-at-home moms should have to trade lives with a single working mother. I don't know if there are any harder working people in the world than single mothers, or in some cases, single working fathers. To work and try to keep track of everything happening without a spouse, that's more difficult than a husband being away on business for a few days. I thank my lucky stars that I have a teammate and we're on the same page. When one is absent, the other steps it up and takes charge.

Having a good marriage and a well-run home life isn't easy, but it can be simple. It's all about the game. View life as a game and your partner as your teammate. Never ever play the game against your partner. As a team, you should share all information. Anytime you withhold information, you're playing against your partner and the game will soon end. If there is ever anything that you are doing and can't tell your spouse, then truly, you shouldn't be doing it. You're playing against them and it will be game over, the pendulum has swung and will only come back if you communicate.

You knew when you picked up this book that it was going to be a commentary on social issues, well, what were you thinking?

Politics and Government: A House Divided

A house divided by itself cannot stand! I know this is in the bible somewhere and though I'm not sure of its exact location, it holds true regardless.

I'm so sick of both parties working desperately to spin every minute detail on each other that the next politician I see in person, I'm going to stick my finger down my throat and puke on them as they pass.

How is it that out of 300 million people in this country we can't find anyone better to lead us? Really, are our choices going to continue to be the guy that can smile the best and promise the most and speak somewhat eloquently?

We so need to change the way we vote in this country. I'm all for the idea that if you are late on your taxes or don't pay any taxes, you don't get a vote. I'm not so sure that this would really be a deterrent though, so many people who do pay taxes still don't vote. Are you sick, lazy, or just plain stupid? If you really think that your vote doesn't count for anything and that it's all a conspiracy where someone behind the scenes decides who will run the country, then I have to tell you…pull your head out of your ass and check in with reality!

When I say that we need to change the way voting is done, I'm serious. Here are some things I think need to replace the current voting rules:

- You have to have an IQ test done and prove that you're of semi-intelligence.

- Your reading comprehension has to be at a ninth-grade level or better. I'd ask for a higher grade, but to be honest, I think this would really cut down, probably by 50 percent, the amount of people that would get to vote.

- You can't vote for a candidate just because you agree with him on one issue (such as abortion or global warming). At the polls you have to know the issues and vote by them. After you're done choosing where you stand on all issue, the candidate that is closest to the number of issues you're in favor of is your choice for president.

- No one but Congress knows who is running. Each candidate is assigned a letter (ten candidates labeled by letters A–J). You vote by the letter. Remember the TV show *The Dating Game?* We need a presidential game show.

- There is no party recognition, Republicans or Democrats. This way, you are forced to vote on the issues.

- There is no on stage debating. No candidate can criticize their opponent by bringing up past votes from twenty years ago. I give a rat's ass if a politician voted for war ten years ago, but now avoids it. Things change and aging/maturing does make a difference in your views later on.

- No candidate can raise funds for their campaign. The government allots $30 million to each candidate and their advertisements can only depict them by their letter, not their name. Computerized voices must be implemented when advertising verbally and must be spoken through a source that is not the candidate...this way, no recognized speech or slang terms can be pinpointed as to the candidate's real identity.

- The candidate must have a strong business background.

This really wouldn't be too difficult to pull off. There are other things I would implement regarding a politician's time in office. Yeah, there might already be term limits in place, but what I will discuss later is a hell of a lot more productive for the country and the states.

I truly am so blown away by the fact that just having a few really good leaders could make the economy better than all the laws and talk. I'm sorry, but I really haven't seen anyone in office the likes of a five-star general. Why did Patton have to die? We need a leader with confidence to say, "Get your crap together or get the hell out of my way." We need someone who won't pansy ass down to the population.

We need someone who can say, "You know what, Joe Public, you may not like it, but this is business and you don't have a clue what the hell you're talking about." Then they proceed to make changes that truly do right by the country.

I want a politician that when he learns the crime rate is up in Los Angeles by 20 percent, he gets on the phone, calls the chief of police and cusses him out and lets the chief know in as few words as possible, "If you can't fix it, I'll find someone that will!" That's a real politician in my eyes.

So, I'm still shocked, and mind you, I don't want to throw our recent presidential candidates leaders under the bus, but with all the great retired CEOs and CFOs that ran great and huge companies in this country, you're telling me that we can't get someone to square things away in a professional business-like manner? I'm totally dumbfounded on this. This is the best we can do? We have 300 million people in this country and this is all we can find?

Jack Welch, who ran a company called General Electric, used a business consulting firm that had solutions. The company is named Six Sigma and there is a great book about it. Through Six Sigma, GE was turned upside down and right-side up. They measured everything and anything that was a representation of the company. Managers were put through classes that made them black-belts in their divisions. Why can't we hire Six Sigma Consulting to measure and change everything, to teach our "leaders/ politicians" how to run this country with knowledge that truly works?

One of the biggest lessons in business is to make sure you always have the right people on your team. This means, if you have five people that don't give a rat's ass about making things better for the company, you get them off of the train and replace them with people who do want to improve the company or agree with the leader of the company's direction. You might say that the our government is doing this. The government is loading the train with the people who agree with their ideology and that is unfortunately driving us closer to socialism. You can call me paranoid, but I will show you by the end of this chapter how close we are to socialism.

Each and every year that I watch the candidates begin their quest for the office of president, I can't help but to notice how friendly they get with Hollywood or religion. Politicians aren't completely stupid, they know that if they can rub elbows with someone famous they will be considered cool. Bill Clinton showed us how cool he was to blow his horn on Jay Leno's show. Big F'n deal! Then he's getting close to the religious leaders of the day because as a politician he knows he needs the votes. Who better to hobnob with to get thousands upon thousands of un-questioned votes? It's unfortunate that churchgoers will do what their pastor tells them and won't think for themselves.

Fast forward a few years and Bill's horn isn't the only thing getting blown...did we hear anything from the congregation that backed him during the run for presidency...um, NO!

Hey sheeples, learn about the issues and vote on them, not on what you're told to do by some cheatin' Jimmy

Swaggert type. There are usually a dozen other issues than abortion; pull your head out and read, educate yourself and vote with knowledge of the facts.

The presidency has become a Hollywood reality show. It's all about who looks the best, speaks most eloquently, and can make promises to the idiot voters, people who want a bunch of handouts.

I'm serious, maybe we do need to have a higher council made up of ten or twelve business executives that can manage the country. Oh wait! We have that, don't we! It's called Congress. Wow! I just realized that the movie *Star Wars* had a council. Isn't it sad that a movie has a better version of reality than we can manifest in the real world? This one-man-running-a-country thing just isn't working out.

Every year it seems that things get worse and worse, no matter which side has a president in the office. A house divided by itself cannot stand… This is true for one's own personal sake too. If you're divided within about something it's going to show in your work, your friendships, and everything around you. Welcome to America and get a glimpse of the personalities on TV as they work to spin each other's side into being completely wrong about everything. The worse thing is that, like the sheeple of the church, there is a sheeple of the parties, Republicans and Democrats alike. Sheeple do what they're told and believe everything they hear from their leaders.

Imagine if you had a leader of a company that really didn't care about his job or the company. The only thing this leader wanted to do was to stand up in front of everyone, smile, and say something that made him sound important.

The leader kept telling his people that tomorrow would be a brighter day and then he gave them things that they didn't deserve, basically buying their love and affection... or...getting their vote, to be re-elected. It sounds quite foolish and that a company with a leader such as this would surely fail the company. Well, welcome to America.

Do you want proof? Some of our leaders said that they really didn't understand the health bill that was placed before them, but said, "We've got to pass it and then we'll figure it out." How long would your company last if you just spent millions or billions of dollars before you even knew why or what you were spending it on? Exactly! It's a stupid frame of mind that acts before understanding. Here, let me jump off of this bridge and then somewhere along the way down, I'll think about why I'm jumping.

I'm a firm believer that with all the bickering between the two biggest parties, that if someone intelligent came along, that was decent looking, could speak well, and was running as an Independent, he'd win hands down. I think there is a third party because one day, we will truly need representation from someone that doesn't bicker night and day, but can rationally think their way out of the proverbial box. The parties have become like two little kids that need to be separated and sent to the nearest corner for a long-overdue time out.

While we're at it, changing the way politicians are voted for, let's make some changes to the politician's job. Let's use a governor for our examples.

- Everything is tracked and measured regarding the politician's job. He has a term limit, but if the data shows he's not making great strides in a positive nature for the public, then he is out.

- If the politician enters the office with his state in debt (example $40 billion in debt) then he has a five-year limit to made strides in lowering that debt. If the debt is higher after two years…kicked to the curb.

- The government pays for everything he personally and honestly needs while in office. At the end of his five-year term, if he reaches set goals, he gets a huge bonus. (Example: if he decreases that $40b. debt to $15b., the bonus is $10mil.)

- After term is up and new guy comes in, if after two years the debt is going back up, then the old guy returns with a signing bonus and a bigger bonus to match if he reaches the set goals as done previously.

- Get rid of all lobbyists. If a politician meets with a lobbyist, even through a friend, they're out of office.

- There is no special retirement plan for politicians. When they leave office they are no longer paid. Like any citizen, they must invest their money properly for retirement. Just because they were a politician doesn't mean they should collect for the rest of their lives.

Would a politician spend $20 million on something if he knew he wasn't going to get his bonus at the end of his term? I don't think so. We've got to get politicians that are smart businessmen first and not some smooth-talking con artist that will eventually make headlines on the front page of the newspaper week after week.

If you ever get a chance, go to YouTube.com and watch the videos on Milton Friedman, an economic advisor to President Reagan. The man is unbelievably intelligent and if you can recall TV talk show personality Phil Donahue, you'll see a very clear and concise dialogue concerning libertarianism and the education to those who don't recognize what socialism really means, but blindly follow along while thinking that I'm out of bounds with my fear of losing the country I love. Check out some of the platform of the Libertarian Party.

- **Personal Liberty**
  Individuals should be free to make choices for themselves and to accept responsibility for the consequences of the choices they make. No individual, group, or government may initiate force against any other individual, group, or government. Our support of an individual's right to make choices in life does not mean that we necessarily approve or disapprove of those choices.
- **Personal Relationships**
  Sexual orientation, preference, gender, or gender identity should have no impact on the government's treatment of individuals, such as in current marriage, child custody, adoption, immigration or military service laws. Government does not have the authority to define, license or restrict personal relationships. Consenting adults should be free

to choose their own sexual practices and personal relationships.

- **Economic Liberty**
  Libertarians want all members of society to have abundant opportunities to achieve economic success. A free and competitive market allocates resources in the most efficient manner. Each person has the right to offer goods and services to others on the free market. The only proper role of government in the economic realm is to protect property rights, adjudicate disputes, and provide a legal framework in which voluntary trade is protected. All efforts by government to redistribute wealth, or to control or manage trade, are improper in a free society
- **Government Finance and Spending**
  All persons are entitled to keep the fruits of their labor. We call for the repeal of the income tax, the abolishment of the Internal Revenue Service and all federal programs and services not required under the U.S. Constitution. We oppose any legal requirements forcing employers to serve as tax collectors. Government should not incur debt, which burdens future generations without their consent. We support the passage of a "Balanced Budget Amendment" to the U.S. Constitution, provided that the budget is balanced exclusively by cutting expenditures, and not by raising taxes.

Our government needs a time out. Our politicians need a nap. It is never okay for the heads of state to run a business such as healthcare. It's never okay for the government to mettle in the affairs of capitalism. The government's only place in the lives of the American people is to be a watchful parent and make sure that a third party, such as you or I, are not taken advantage of or encroached upon by a more powerful entity. The government's role is to let people do what they will do and be ready to react when someone puts the life of another human being at risk. As an example: It's not the government's right to set helmet laws for the motorcycle riders. It's not the government's role to make sure you have health insurance. It's not the government's role to make sure your child has a lunch ticket at school. It's not the government's role to own any land other than where their buildings are located. The only thing the government was made up to do was to assist in protecting the rights of its citizens

On a side note: Has anyone noticed that many of the states that are bankrupt are run by liberals?

It is right for the government to mandate all drivers have auto insurance. Why? Because, in the case that someone is injured by another party, there is a responsibility to that injured party. Again, the government is the parent and just tells us which corner to go to until things are settled or agreed upon. Everything else should be returned to the public sector.

There are billions upon billions of dollars being spent by the government that is a total waste of time. For instance: They will never be able to create safety in the airline travel industry. They try by setting regulations, but they truly have no control. If a mechanic were to screw up and leave a wrench somewhere that blocks the landing gears from proper use, how has the government created safety? They haven't. I'm not trying to scare anyone from traveling, I'm just saying, the government is made up of people with the same type of faults you or I have. Safety truly is an illusion.

When has government ever run a well-organized business? The politicians can't even handle running the government in the black, how the hell are they going to run healthcare efficiently? They won't! They can't! The government needs to stay out of private industry and agree to be a silent observer in order to make laws that protect its citizens and nothing more.

If you want to be a socialist, move to Cuba. You want to know why you won't move to Cuba? You won't move because you enjoy the freedom that capitalism has given you. A government running all industry leads to poverty. In that respect, I now know why so many people are agreeing with socialism: it's because they're too lazy to get up and do something about their lives, their financial situations.

Why do you think most wealthy people don't want a national healthcare system? Because they know it will cost them more in the long run, it won't be run well, and it's an unjust method to control lives…it stifles a person's freedom.

When was the last time the government made a fine-running automobile? They haven't! The government didn't come up with the idea of an assembly line to crank out cars and make our country grow and prosper. Henry Ford made that happen because of one word, CAPITALISM! Now we seem to have government-run capitalism (socialism).

So, we've established that the government hasn't done anything in the way of business that has really done any good for the country. Well, let me take that back; the government of the last eighty or so years. Good ol' George and the gang would be rolling in their graves right now if they knew they fought and died for people to lose their rights to a socialist.

Do you want more proof that we're moving into a socialist realm? The president fired the CEO of GM the day before giving them bailout money. What right does a president have in firing anyone in the private sector? I didn't know that our government or the president owned GM. Yeah, it's time to be scared.

It seems that the only two things that have gotten any better in this world are science and technology. Hurray!! Social standards have gotten worse across the board, but my main concern is when the government is going to take over those two industries. Imagine Albert Einstein sitting in a lab all day long, getting paid to just sit there and think. If he doesn't produce anything significant, he still gets paid. Can you imagine how many people are going to instantly become scientists when the government socializes that industry?

Where is the puppet-master? You know, the guy behind the scene pulling the strings? I just want to know how it is that all this crap can happen to a country that is supposed to be a superpower and run the world. I think the Tea Party is on to something big. They are a group demanding the return of our rights as citizens. They want less government involvement in their lives. They want fewer taxes taken out of their pay. They want our forefathers to be proud of the country they fought for. One of the things I really learned by watching news station personalities call the Tea

Party people names like lunatics or crazies, is that the news stations are controlled completely by the government, or are at least in cahoots with daddy G.

You might say that's preposterous, the news is not controlled. Then tell me, why does each news channel report the same exact issues almost to the minute? They're scripted worse than any sitcom show you could imagine.

Control what people hear and see and you sway the minds of America. Does anyone find it incredible that our standards of education are not the highest in the world? Why not? Again, socialism has crept its ugly little ass into the classroom. Education needs to be privatized and people need to pay for their kids to go to school. Even if it was only thirty bucks a month, it'd be worth it. I bet then all parents would make sure their little Henry isn't texting in class. If a parent has to pay for their kid to be in school, they're damn sure going to make sure they're getting their dollars' worth.

There's just too much going on in a very bad way and people aren't making intelligent decisions. When we won't vote for a businessman such as Mitt Romney, who is very freaking good at business in a great way, because he is a Mormon, or we ridicule someone like Howard Dean because he gets a yelp in his voice during an exciting moment and instead we go for someone because of the way they look or can blow an instrument, while being blown, then we as a country need to revamp the way we operate.

The role of government needs to be cut in half. People need to join the Tea Party. Though I'm not a big fan of Facebook, I'll tell you why it's so important to our country. If we're not careful, a socialist government (ours) will take it over and remove all the power of the people. With Facebook, if you were a member of the Tea Party, the leader could call to arms everyone across the country in a matter of minutes. If they wanted to protest something, then within a half hour a thousand Tea Party members from every state across the country could be sitting on the steps of their state's capital. No phone calls telling its members to move now. Just one sentence with a location and a click of the mouse on a send button and bam! The next thing you know, protests at every state capital across the country. That is power in the hands of the people. Let's see the news stations call them crazy now. As a matter of fact, the Tea Party should show up in droves at the front door of every news station across the country to prove their power in communication.

The role of government today thinks that they need to fix everything for everyone. Here is how close we came to closing the doors permanently in this country. The bailouts, if they didn't happen, could have shut us down completely, from superpower to zero power. The companies that got bailed out were too large to be allowed to fail. The real communication is that if they had failed, we were kaput.

It would have been unfortunate, but by hitting zero, we would have had to really wake up. In other words, the government, in its weak state, decided to administer a drug to the addict. Like a parent trying to help their child fight the addiction, the government didn't let the child fail and in truth hurt everyone.

You might reply, yeah, but they saved thousands from being unemployed. The truth is, they saved thousands from being embarrassed by their addiction to greed. Those companies needed to fail like an addict needs to hit rock bottom before they can get any better.

Bottom line, government needs to get out of the way and let capitalism progress and create great lives as it normally does. America has a broken balance sheet and we need to fix it. Can you believe we're talking about bailing out the public pensions? There are retired workers in their forties getting six-figure retirement benefits. Who thought that was a good idea and could sustain itself?

If a handful of companies not getting bailed out could have buried the country, how close to the edge are we still? Has capitalism slowed down because, going back to a previous chapter, we've let our kids grow up with the frame of mind that nobody wins or loses? Socialists don't have to win or lose because everything is taken care of for them. They don't have to care. They don't have to participate to be taken care of. Where the hell is the story of the little red hen today—teaching about a good work ethic and personal initiative?

Other countries may be using socialist rules and just getting by on a somewhat okay basis, but they aren't really doing any better than us in the long run; at least, not if we decide to get better and regain our power. Our country needs leaders that can stand up and say no to the socialist and that can also say no to the whiners. Our country and its leaders needs to grow a pair of balls that would make our forefathers proud.

Before we can do anything in this country to make it better, we have to have the people in power not do things for their own benefit. These people should be instantly kicked out of their cushy little seat. When you read what

I'm about to share, I think you'll agree. This is a post that has gone around the Internet and though it's been floating around for years, I have to ask, why isn't anything being done about it? Here it is, in all its facts and glory:

"For too long we have been too complacent about the workings of Congress. Many citizens had no idea that Congress members could retire with the same pay after only one term, that they didn't pay into Social Security, that they specifically exempted themselves from many of the laws they have passed (such as being exempt from any fear of prosecution for sexual harassment) while ordinary citizens must live under those laws. The latest is to exempt themselves from the Healthcare Reform that is being considered...in all of its forms. Somehow, that doesn't seem logical. We do not have an "elite group" that is above the law. I truly don't care if they are Democrat, Republican, Independent or whatever. The self-serving must stop. This is a good way to do that.

Proposed 28th Amendment to the United States Constitution:

"Congress shall make no law that applies to the citizens of the United States that does not apply equally to the Senators and/or Representatives; and, Congress shall make no law that applies to the Senators and/or Representatives that does not apply equally to the citizens of the United States."

If that's not eye-opening enough for you, then let me share this tidbit. I think it puts the nail in the coffin and clearly demonstrates how our country is being run by idiots.

"Let me get this straight. We're going to be gifted with a health care plan written by a committee whose chairman says he doesn't understand it, passed by a Congress that hasn't read it but exempts themselves from it, to be signed by a president who also hasn't read it and who smokes, with funding administered by a treasury chief who didn't pay his taxes, to be overseen by a surgeon general who is obese, and financed by a country that's broke. What the hell could possibly go wrong?" —origin unknown

Since GM is no longer known as General Motors, but Government Motors, in our socialist state, we should mention something here about unions and how outdated they are. I'm sure it must come to pass that if the new GM is going to give handouts by saving jobs, then they need to also give handouts to the American people who are supposed to truly be the owners of GM…since this is a government of the people and they were our tax dollars.

Union people can work from the age of twenty to forty-five and retire with huge pensions and full benefits, yet the government is making the people of this country work to sixty-five—hmmm. Unions are always asking for less work and more money. There was a time that unions were needed to keep things fair in this country, but now, with the youth of today, it's proven that the youth won't work if they don't like the conditions. To further things along, why should I have an extra \$2500–\$3500 applied to my purchase of a new automobile just so someone can get benefits later on? If the new GM is going to let this happen then they should make sure everyone in every company across America gets the same benefit. Imagine paying \$1000 dollars for your burger at McDonald's because their retirees need benefits.

Unions at this stage of the game are bringing down our standard of living. It seems that to the unions, a janitor should now earn $100K annually because a union contract says so. I'm sure the dollar amount is an exaggeration, but not by much. Unions are throwing off the economy and making it harder for the American public to purchase goods and services. I go back to the points made previously that people should be paid on a commission basis or some standard that creates a raise when the job is done correctly, not just because some contract says it has to be done.

I know if I buy a car that is considered a lemon, that there is a law enabling me to get a replacement or my money back. What about my time spent and the interest I could have gotten if I'd left that money in an interest-bearing account? Shouldn't I get something from this union member that didn't do his job right...perhaps because it was a Monday?

Now that we're moving into being socialists instead of being capitalists, which is how this country first became great, there needs to be compensation for those of us who have paid more than a fair share and hustled our way through without unions protecting us if we had done any shoddy work. Come on big daddy G, gimme gimme gimme! If you can afford to bail out unionized companies then you need to bailout everyone. Oh wait! That's what you're doing already.

So tell me, are you starting to see some kind of pattern in the irresponsibility of our elected officials? I sure the hell am. It's time America wakes up; though, after you read the next few chapters you may wonder if America is doomed. Now get out there and vote!

What Happened to Good Ol' Sloppy Joe?

Now I've heard it all. Life in this country is not hard for kids. I heard a person talking about how tough kids have it these days. My ass! The reason I get so pissed when people talk about how tough the kids have it these days is because they're being trained to complain and believe that life is tough. How can these kids grow up and think anything is possible if all they hear is how tough it is? They're taught that grade school is hard, high school is hard, college is hard, work is hard, retirement is hard, death is hard. It seems like kids of the day are racking their brains to come up with things to worry or be depressed about. They haven't even started paying taxes! What's so depressing? Some parents act like their kids get waterboarded all day long.

How about if we start informing the kids that life is great and actually things are pretty good. On a side note: I was just wondering, not that it's bad by any means, but why do kids go out to eat sushi with their parents and not get things like sloppy Joe, chipped beef on toast, or Hamburger Helper? What happened to that part of our youth?

Back to the lecture at hand, what's so tough about having the opportunity to play sports? What's so tough about getting up for school where they've actually been doing more socializing than studying? What's so tough about having summers off? What's so tough about getting a license at sixteen? What's so tough about playing games? What's so tough about eating candy and ice cream? Being a kid is supposed to be great...play some sports, get good grades, hang with your friends. Is there something I'm missing? Is there a big deal or are we making it a big deal? What so tough for kids these days?

If the person was referring to the rules that kids are supposed to follow, again...what's so tough? If little Steven steals a car today, the first offense can be three months of juvenile hall, whereas, back in the sixties, seventies, and eighties it was just six months of probation and a slap on the hand. If a kid has some sort of medicine in his locker at school, he can be suspended, whereas again, back in the day, if this happened, the principle might ask if you are sick and want to go home. By the way, I think the way things were handled back in the day were better, but the new way of handling things doesn't make it tough to be a kid.

What's so tough about following rules? Am I a stickler for rules? To be fair—yes and no. If you can't tell everyone what you're doing, perhaps you shouldn't be doing it. I may be caught up in thought and drive a little faster than a posted speed limit. If I get caught, I don't expect the rules to be bent for me, I should have been paying better attention.

Life is not hard if you just accept that you may have screwed up. Life is not hard if you get with the program and do what is required or, if appropriate, when asked. Don't tell me kids have it hard today when they're living in the same world as me. Oh wait, they're not!

The kids I'm talking about are under the age of eighteen and live at home with their parent/s. They may have some simple chores such as taking out the trash or doing the dishes, but did they get to eat? Do they have clothes on their back? Is there a roof over their head and food in their stomach? Again, how hard is it on kids these days? I'd think I'd died and gone to heaven if someone was supplying these basic needs for me each day. Don't forget that these kids have cell phones, Xbox, Playstation, DS, etc. I remember a time when kids were lucky to play Pong, Pitfall, or Frogger on Atari. Then you'd throw your football pads on your handlebars and ride your ass to junior football.

It appears that there are some kids over the age of eighteen who are still living at home on their parent/s' dime. Someone might say, "It's tough on kids these days because the job market is down and they can't find work to support themselves." There are so many ways to make money while waiting for the "perfect" job to come along. Get out and wash cars, mow lawns, teach the elderly how to use a computer.

I hate to break it to the younger generation, but Microsoft or Goldman Sachs isn't going to knock on your door and ask if you'd like to earn $100K in their office. Go make something happen. Make yourself busy. Good things come from being active. You might be washing the car of someone who owns a company and is looking for good, young talent and is impressed that you're working your tail off. Go make your own luck.

One of my friends has a son in junior college. The kid has an auto detail business and makes more money part-time than his older buddies who found work with the mainstream-type jobs—mall work, clothing stores, fast-food. The kid pulls down $200 in four hours while his buddies work all day and make $50. Kids don't have it tough—at least, not the ones that take the initiative to do something with their lives regardless of what others think is the path to follow. There are so many things kids can do to make big money, but they've been taught to depend on mom and dad.

Maybe we should take some of these college kids, give them $500 bucks cash and drop them in some rough, poverty-stricken, third-world country and then we tell them, "Good luck. Use that education we paid for to make your life happen." I wonder how many kids would be sharp enough to not spend the limited amount of money on crap like a chocolate caramel double foaming latte.

Kids don't know what tough is. Rarely do they ever experience it. Live in parts of Africa where babies are dying daily of famine...that's tough! Live where a weapon is thrown in your hands by the age of seven and you're forced to kill or be killed. Vietnam wasn't that long ago, imagine getting that call to go to Vietnam whether you wanted to or not. That's tough! When little Steven can go from his bedroom to the kitchen, open the fridge and get a snack, he's privileged.

I think a lot of people and parents push the idea of life being hard or tough because they may not have experienced a whole lot of success. I never hear my successful friends complain about being super busy day in and day out. Like the complainers, they have to deal with work and family issues, but they do what they do and push through. People who say life is tough have no momentum or willpower to change their circumstances, so they project these thoughts onto their kids. How sad is that?

I tell my kids that life is easy if you work it right. There's nothing difficult about it if you tackle it head on and push through. The only time it's tough is when you're not allowed to participate of your own accord. If you're in America, you've got no excuse.

Who or what are you comparing your life to that you think it's so tough? You might be paying rent on a doublewide while someone else is paying a mortgage on a two-story home, but still, no one is living for free. The difference in your dwelling has all to do with your choices, not how tough you think something is. Funny, but not so funny is the fact that the more you preach or take these types of victimizing actions, the more you project onto your kids. Eventually they'll believe you and keep the vicious cycle of pity-party-seekers alive through their own kids. Congratulations, you proved yourself right.

Things I Hate Because I Can

I am being as honest as possible in this book of mine. So, I guess it's okay for me to list things that I truly hate in life. Besides, I need to fill up space. Enjoy!

Let's start with:

Jared from Subway—I can't stand the look on his face in those commercials. I hate the way he chews!

Jean shorts (jorts) on guys.

Mustaches or beards—Still trying to figure those out in today's world. Go pick up a *People* or *US Weekly* magazine. Do you see any mustaches in there? Are you Kenny Loggins?

Smokers—Sorry, stinky, all the perfume or cologne isn't going to cover up the fact that you stink. Also, when you throw your cigarette butts out of the car window, it really is littering.

People who aren't ready with their change at a toll booth—
You've only had five warning signs that you were approach-
ing the toll booth, idiot!

ATM machines that ask about language—You're in
America, speak English or at least understand it if you're a
tourist.

Greeting cards filled with glitter—It's like a bomb filled
with Agent Orange that goes all over me, my clothes, and
my house.

The guys that wipe their boogers on the wall above the
men's urinal in the bathroom. Really...are you a caveman?
What makes a guy want to wipe a booger on the wall when
there's toilet paper or paper towels readily available?

Men that wear cologne at the gym. It's a fitness club, not a
night club.

When people sing the national anthem in their own way at
a sporting event.

People at the airports that stop in the middle of the halls
to look at the screens. I smash my luggage into theirs every
chance I get and watch their bag spin off into the sunset.

The cab drivers that don't have change for a twenty-dollar
bill. Do you think I'm so dumb that I'm going to give you
a huge tip?

I can't stand when people put their own names on the back of professional team jerseys.

Cell phones hooked onto the belt. It's not an accessory and you're not Batman.

When people jam themselves onto the elevator before others have a chance to exit.

Fanny packs.

When baseball players get hurt sliding into a base—go play football, hockey, boxing, or MMA, then come tell me about your slide.

The new eco-friendly water bottles that spill every time you open them. I think I might sue.

Dr. Phil—Just for being Dr. Phil.

When grown men use " :) " in an email or a text.

Ladies that say, "I'm going to put on my face" (in regards to wearing makeup).

The kids from Barney that are over-acting. This was banned from my house a looooong time ago.

People who describe food as "To die for." I've yet to eat a food that I would be willing to kill myself over.

1-800 customer service lines that don't give customer service.

The Kate–plus-eight short haircut. She looks like Sonic from the video game.

Jon and Kate-plus-eight—they're famous for being famous? What the hell have they ever done?

When people mess up and say, "My bad."

When trainers at the gym do the sexy after-workout stretch with the MILFS, yet never do it with the non-cougars.

Veggie chili…what's the point?

Over-the-top end-zone dancing in football. Be like Barry Sanders and act like you've been there before and you'll be there a lot more in the future.

Shirts that say, "Give blood, play rugby."

The way my pee smells after eating asparagus.

Stickers on the back windows of trucks with the Calvin kid pissing on a Ford or Chevy.

When guys hold their sunglasses on the back of their head.

When I order a burger and they put onions or pickles on the side, though I didn't order it that way, yet they charge me more for it.

The wiggles.

People with long, dirty nails.

Fat people with tiny cars and a license plate that says, "Cutie."

The Taco Bell manager that acts like he's running a hedge fund and berates his eighteen-year-old employees.

People who smack their lips when they eat.

Black Friday—The day after Thanksgiving where everyone loses every bit of sense they have and go crazy by shopping and trampling one another and then the news reports about it every year.

When a bartender uses one of those "measured pour" devices for the exact ounce of liquor. Can't the bartender be in charge for Christ's sake?

When people lick their finger to turn the pages.

Tramp stamp tattoos on the lower backs on guys.

When people split the check at lunch and break it down to the penny and say things like, "I had one less Coke than everyone else."

People that still pay by check at the grocery store and hold up the lines.

People who say TGIF.

People who answer, "Doing okay for a Monday."

People who won't let a car over in traffic just so they can stay one car ahead.

When people throw their gum on the sidewalk. Hey, jerk, have you noticed all the black rubbery marks. That's why gum has been banned in Singapore.

Feliz Navidad
Happy Rosh Hashanah
Merry Stressmas
Happy Holidays

P ick a freakin' salutation and stick with it! Why aren't we allowed to say Merry Christmas anymore without someone getting offended. I literally catch myself not wanting to offend anyone and having to think whether I should say happy this or happy that instead of Merry Christmas. Usually I come up with the old standby...Happy Holidays. You know it's getting bad out there in the world when you have to worry about offending someone by being nice. I'll often go to multiple card stores to find the least offensive and nicest holiday card. It's insane!

It's not that I mind greeting someone with their native salutation, but why do some get offended when I greet with what I grew up with? Merry Christmas, sometimes it just slips out.

Mind you, I enjoy the Christmas season and all that it's supposed to stand for, thankfulness and giving, and the fact that someone is wishing me anything nice during this stressful time of the year is happily accepted. I just want to know how anyone can be offended by my saying Merry Christmas.

Christmas, in itself, is a helluva time to people watch. During this time of year it's interesting to ask someone how they're doing and before I know it, I'm getting play-by-play details of their Christmas shopping. Some are all stressed out while maxing out their credit cards while others are in a panic to get the perfect toy that is all the rage.

Maybe we need to step back and really ask what Christmas is all about. Why is it so stressful? Why are people fighting over what they think is the perfect gift? Why aren't people more relaxed at this time of the year? Really, the year is just about over and things are coming to a close, which leaves new and exciting things to plan for in the coming New Year.

I can't even wish someone a Merry Christmas without them being offended. Seriously, when I'm in the store or somewhere that I run across someone I know, I've had to stop and think about what to wish them…Can I say Merry Christmas? Nope, I better say Happy Holidays!

You know what Christmas is supposed to be about; it's about the idea of Santa Claus for the little kids, setting up the house with lights, the tree with ornaments, listening to Christmas music, or watching *A Christmas Story* on the all-day TV loop with my family. It's a truly great feeling. I try to not go overboard when it comes to the presents and just want to share the time with family and friends.

I think, even more than Christmas, my favorite holiday of the year is Thanksgiving. No one is stressed except the woman making dinner for a thousand guests. Around my home, I savor the smell of my family's cooking and hanging around the house with my wife, kids, and all of our family in the area. When friends and family show up I'm beside myself with the knowledge that it doesn't get any better than this...least not at this time of the year. Think about it...tons of food, beer, football, more food, kids running around the neighborhood like crazy...the good life.

Really, this is the time for letting go of old family squabbles or rocky relationships and just share with the ones you're with the joy of life and the things you can be thankful for.

Whether it's Thanksgiving or Christmas, let go of the need to be offended and step up to gratitude for what you do have. There will always be someone who thinks you've got it made compared to them. As a matter of fact, there's probably someone right now, this very minute, putting a lawsuit together against some major department store because the Santa they had taking wish lists from little kids didn't deliver and now little Stevie's feelings are hurt.

On one hand we're the melting pot of the world and on the other we're not allowed to be whom we originally were. So, for the sake of our country and the proverbial jingle-balls it needs, I'm bringing back Merry Christmas right here and right now.

Ho! Ho! Ho! Happy Holidays and a big jolly fat-man of a Merry Christmas!

A Race Is for Speed, Not Color

There are no more excuses for a tough life. One of the things I find amazing in this so called "tough" life is the race card. I completely forget a person is white, black, Mexican, Jewish, Italian, Polish, Middle-Eastern, or any other race/culture until they remind me. Really, how much longer is society going to play the race card? It's really getting old. We're in the F'n melting pot of the world. Have you taken the time to notice that every race/culture has its problems? Do you remember Hitler and the Jews?

Is my life tough because my ancestors were forced to hard labor when they came to America from Italy? Not really! Do I expect to get special treatment now because my ancestors were treated poorly a hundred years ago? Do I expect to get special treatment because I was born with greasy hair and a big power schnoz? No, I don't!

Are there people in the world who hate you for the color of your skin? Sure, but they're idiots. Prove them wrong by rising above it. Don't be offended because you got arrested as a black man in a white neighborhood, because truth be known, most white people could care less what color anyone is in this day in age. Are there going to be cops who engage in racial profiling? Yes, but again, they're idiots.

As I covered earlier, many of them only have high school diplomas and are in the career for all the wrong reasons to begin with.

If you're not doing anything wrong, no matter the color of your skin, then you have nothing to worry about. Let the idiot cop go about his business and you'll be on your way. Don't take it personally; you're not the one with the problem…unless you keep harping on it.

I'm sure I'm going to catch some grief for that last paragraph, but really, if I do, then you're harping. I could care less what color you are, move on, life's not that tough.

Race and culture are two things we have to let go of already. I think it gets the world into more trouble by trying to recognize someone's background. It helps to enable a person of color—and yes, white is a color also—to have a pity party if someone looks at them the wrong way.

Have you really stopped to check how much you're physically hurting when someone uses a racial slur aimed at you? Is your mind so weak that it caves in at the slightest hint of a racial tone? Come on, people, stop being so offended because of the color of your skin or the culture from which you were born into.

I don't bitch and moan because I'm an Italian, I bitch and moan because I can. I don't bitch and moan because I'm white and have listened to other races throw out the racial card of prejudice bias. I'm white and was born that way. No one ever told me while growing up, "Hey Vince, you're white, you've got the greatest gig going." No one ever told me, "Hey Vince, because you're white you're going to automatically be successful over the other races." It just doesn't happen that way.

Somewhere along the line there is a lesson taught through observation or lecture. Some people see or hear the lesson and interpret for themselves or fall into the belief that what they saw or heard was automatically right. The lesson is how to use the race card.

There are many great people who never once used the race card, though they may have been judged on race or culture. These people could care less what others are saying. These people go about their business and make their life happen regardless of the color of their skin or the culture they were born in. I applaud these people immensely.

If you've ever listened to the lie, "You just can't get ahead because you're of the wrong color," and if you believed it, then you are meant to be where you are today. Where you are today could actually have worked out well for you if you were taught to force your way through prejudice. Maybe you stand in front of a pulpit to remind people that their race has been put down and now needs to fight to regain respect. If that's so, then you're sending the wrong message. There is no one being held down today because of race. There might be a few instances here and there of racial profiling, but again, it's an idiot behind the act...let it go!

Stop Making Out with Your Cat!

For years I've seen and heard people talk about their animals like they are their kids. "Oh my little doggie woggie, want to go for a walk? Come here and give mommy a kiss." Are you serious? Do you know where that dog's mouth has been? Licking his ass I'm sure! And, if not that, then definitely licking his balls.

The other day I was on a plane and sitting next to a woman holding her dog. Do I really want to sit next to someone with a dog? NO! There are other people just as allergic to dogs. You can't just assume that everyone is fine with you bringing your dog on the plane. Next time I fly I'm going to bring a poison ivy plant, a bag of pollen, some wasps, dust mites, and some mold.

People are getting crazy with their pets. Somewhere along the line they were taught that a dog's mouth was cleaner than a human's. That's crap! Did you know that the number-one reason for infant children having worms in their system is from little puppies licking the infant's face and spreading germs...parasites.

Some people let their grown dogs lick them in the face. Again, wrong action! Not to mention disgusting. A mother dog of newborn puppies often licks up the crap of the puppy...and you think momma dog is just coming to show you some affection. Ha! She just wants you to taste the same poop she's been sticking her nose in.

It amazes me that people have no concept that others might not have the same appreciation for animals. Don't get me wrong, I think animals are great, but because of my allergies, I just can't have them around. If I did have them, they'd have to be outside all the time. They're animals; they have fur coats for that very reason. If left outside their fur would grow thicker no matter the type of dog it is, that's usually known as a winter coat. They're genetically built to survive as an animal…in the outdoors.

You will do what you want and if that means having your dog in the house, obviously, that's your prerogative. If you happen to invite guests over, don't just take it for granted that they feel the same way. Be courteous and put your dog out in the yard while you have guests. I hate it when I'm invited to a friend's house and during dinner their little dog is at my side licking his chops and begging for scraps. I remember one time at a friend's house, my buddy's wife put her plate on the floor for the dog to lick clean after she was finished. I almost barfed. Then there are the times I've seen a cat walk across the dinner table before we're getting ready to sit down and eat. It makes me want to go wash my dish before I even get served, let alone the fact that now I don't want to sit at the table or even take a chance on eating.

Cat hair and dog hair get everywhere and though people think they've vacuumed their place really good, I got news for them…their place stinks. Don't shoot the messenger, I'm liable to say the same thing about a smoker. They've been around the crap so long that their sense of smell is no longer sensitive to the lingering odor that makes me want to leave as quickly as possible.

Hey, there's your hall pass to not have me around... get some animals to stink up your furniture and take up smoking.

Apparently I'm not alone with my feelings towards dogs and cats. I have a friend who likes dogs, but has to immediately wash his hands after petting one on the head. He wants a dog, but says it will never come in the house. He grew up with dogs in the house and says that there is nothing you can do to completely prevent fleas from birthing in your carpets and infesting your home...short of getting rid of the dog. He says his dog will either sleep in a doghouse in the backyard or in the garage on a matt, but never ever be allowed in the house. "It's a dog!"

As I think of people and their animals, one of the things that freaks me out the most is a single guy with a cat or when a guy gets a cat just to appease his girlfriend, talk about being whipped. I haven't really pinpointed why this is weird to me, it just is. What is the fascination with cats anyway?

Why is it when women have finally given up on relationships with men, they become the "cat lady" down the street. You know her, every neighborhood has one. There have even been shows on TV where someone has fifty cats running around their house. Animal protection has to come in and remove dead cats from the rafters above a ceiling and the remains of little kittens less than three weeks old. How are these people being overrun by cats? What good do they think they're doing by letting the cats breed in their run down homes with kitty crap everywhere?

I know it sounds like I really dislike animals, but I don't. I just don't see the point in keeping the possibility of germ infestation in close proximity to my healthy life.

I understand why guys have dogs...dogs are cool, but cats? The only thing I find cool about a cat is when someone drops one from a two-story building and it lands on its feet. Sorry all you cat lovers, not that I find a falling or intentionally dropped cat entertaining, but on a puuurfect four-leg landing, my placard says 10.

Okay, the other question I have is concerning these people who love snakes. Are they in it for the attention? I must admit that I find them a bit morbid. These people so look forward to buying small mice that are specifically raised to be fed to the snakes. I understand that a snake has to eat, but really, the fascination with watching the snake go about its business as it chokes the mouse and then begins to swallow it whole, that's just freaky.

I hear Florida Everglades has a problem with snakes because people are buying the snakes when they're small and then when the snake grows and become uncontrollable they're released into the wild. Sometimes the snakes "mysteriously" escape their cage, get out of the house and after eating the neighbor's little dog, go crawling into the sewer system where they find a way into someone's toilet. It happens all the time, just call any pest control in the state of Florida, you'll see.

Hmmm, maybe there should be a show about a snake who ate a dog, who ate a cat, who ate a mouse and then I wouldn't have anything to bitch about because they'd all be gone...after someone killed the snake to make a new pair of boots.

All the Time in the World Yet Still Does Nothing

How the hell is it that a man with no job has the worst lawn? When you have all day to anything you want and you can't get your fat ass out of bed, something is wrong. Really, here it is: the people who work the most have the manicured lawns and nice cars and are living a pretty damned good life, but of course, they work for it. They enable themselves to pay for the service because they care about things, about order, about life.

Some neighborhoods have people staying home all day, oftentimes unemployed, and yet their places are a mess. Their homes, their apartment buildings, and even complete cities look incredibly filthy. How is this?

Shouldn't there be some kind of law that says if you collect welfare or unemployment that you have to spend half of your Saturday in the service of the city you live? Welfare recipients could sweep, paint over graffiti, wash city vehicles, clean city building windows, or vacuum the offices of the city buildings. Why should people get a free ride on welfare when there are services they could still be doing for a couple of hours per day?

I truly don't think it would be that difficult for a city organizer to have a checklist of people on the dole from welfare and jobs that need to be handled around town. This makes absolute sense. The money might be coming to the cities via federal assistance, but still, that doesn't mean the cities can't use the recipients for work.

Wouldn't it be nice to see your tax dollars are really going for something and that someone is actually having to contribute for those who are really supporting them…the taxpayers!

How beautiful would our country look if this happened? We could have people scrapping gum from sidewalks. We could have groups of welfare and unemployment earners cleaning up and painting ugly neighborhoods. If you take a drive through the country and you come across some desolate areas you'll find properties that are full of junk: discarded washers and dryers, old broken-down cars or tractors, rusted-out refrigerators, and a whole assortment of other crap. Get rid of it, people! Clean it the hell up!

America has become such a lazy nation, everywhere you look there's a new gimmick to make people even lazier that they already are.

I can be sitting on the couch watching my flat-screen TV and the phone rings. I don't even have to turn my head to look at the caller ID. Now, the number of the calling party appears on my TV screen.

Why do we have caller ID? Are we so lazy that we don't want to talk to people? Is it to avoid the marketing callers? Did you know that if you don't answer your phone for those people that your number goes right back into their system as an incomplete call? This only means they'll dial you again and again. Pick up the phone and say, "Sorry, not interested," and hang up. Or, you can do what I do. I get my kids to start crying in the background and all the while we're smiling and quietly laughing because I start to give the marketer the run-around. We actually have a great time doing it...the fake voice, the crying in the background. We try to sell them something in return, it's fun. Caller ID is the biggest scapegoat to not confronting life. Pick up the damn phone and speak your F'n mind!

There are a number of things I can think of concerning people and laziness, and yes, occasionally, I too get caught up in them, but hey, I work my ass off so I earned the right to take some "me" time.

I still go to the gym and when I'm there, I actually work out. I don't do cardio as if I were in a race with a snail, I do it so it gets me to the point that when I'm lazy, I have an actual reason. You'll never catch me at home on the couch eating a Twinkie, watching my TV with a belt around my waste that shocks my abs into shape. I mean, come on! What the hell is that all about? It's like the guy who spends a half hour on a treadmill to burn up two hundred calories and then before leaving the gym he buys a chocolate smoothie that has five hundred calories in it.

Let's go down that road. You know the one. You're watching TV late at night while munching on a bag of chips or leftover pizza. Then you see it, the infomercial with all these hot bodies and people crossing their arms to signify that they've bought the material at hand and it totally changed their lives. So what do you do, you order the workout CDs and after watching them once or twice, they sit on the shelf collecting dust.

There's a reason why these late-night infomercial products sell so well. People have worked all day long and now they're tired and don't want to think. They like the concept of being fit, so they'll let the abdominal belt try to do the work, but rarely does it last as long as the lazy habits already in play.

Talking about late-night munchies, it's incredible to me that people don't care about the food they're putting into their system. Some people eat fast food two or three times a day, every single day. They don't care or even stop to wonder how a whole meal can be cooked in under a minute. They only know that they're pissed off if it takes over a minute to get. How the hell do they do it? Where in their brain are they okay with shoveling crap into their mouths constantly. I wonder how much money all these fast-food places are going to contribute to our new health care system.

If they don't die of clogged arteries, perhaps it'll be due to that great new ten-minute workout one can get from the Shaker. Have you seen this commercial? It makes you feel like you can shake the crap out of this maracas shaker for ten minutes and suddenly be hot and sexy. If you're a woman you may end up looking like Megan Fox. On a side note: Watching that commercial makes me uncomfortable if you know what I mean. I'm sure it was intentionally made for the subconscious sexual innuendo it presents.

Let's just make a list and work our way down. These are all things that contribute to our laziness. To stop you ahead of time, there are a couple of things that I also do. I could care less if you call me a hypocrite, it's my book and I'm allowing myself to be as screwed up as the next guy.

Skate shoes—I know it's just a toy, but kids with wheels in their shoes are just looking to roll in front of traffic somewhere.

The Clapper—is for people who have OCD and have to constantly check the light without getting out of bed.

The Tip Card—is for people either too lazy or too stupid to figure the math out for themselves.

Peapod service—it's when you hate grocery shopping so much that you trust someone to choose your produce for you regardless if the tomatoes are too soft and the bananas are close to black, they bring the groceries to you and interrupt during your favorite TV show. What I really want to know is, if you're too lazy to shop for your own food, who the hell answers your door when they get there?

Child leashes—For the parents who so wanted kids, but didn't want to have to pay attention to them while in the real world.

Shopping for clothing online—You see the model in the store magazine wearing something that looks good on them, but when it's on you, everyone wonders about your taste in clothing.

Online banking—Sure it's a quick shortcut to sending out your bills. It's also a quick route to not feeling the pain of your spending sprees. When you handwrite a check, you get to actually to wonder or try to reminisce about what you bought. Most of the time, you don't even know.

Online dating—You take five minutes out of your day to look at someone and wonder if they're too ugly to be on your arm. When they're just right for you and they call to set up a date, they can't get a hold of you because you don't answer the numbers you don't recognize on your caller ID.

Online breakup services—You can now hire someone to breakup with your girlfriend/boyfriend. That's pretty weak, stop avoiding conflict…just deal with it!

Online personal assistants—Let me tell you/warn you about something…these people are not helping people run a business

Speed dating—People who like to play musical chairs, but with lives rather than furniture. One has three to five minutes to judge whether they think someone is cute enough to go on a date with. I wonder how many of these prospects look like *GQ* or *Maxim* material, but are psycho through and through. No one wants to get rejected anymore so they go by numbers instead of names.

Reality shows—are about people trying to make a million bucks in a game because they're too stupid to do it through business. These people would rather ridicule themselves on TV for viewers who get caught up in the drama. Of course, my favorite reality show is okay to watch because these guys live on the brink of death in the Bering Sea, *Deadliest Catch*.

Wikipedia—if we want to know about anything we no longer buy a book and take the time to read about it in depth. Now we just Google it or use Wikipedia.

Kindle—It has turned libraries into meat markets for old folks. Get a book in as little as sixty seconds and still never finish reading it.

Instant messaging—We've gone from writing letters to emails, texting, and other IMs. If you don't get a reply right away they think you're avoiding them.

Music downloads—are quick and easy and you can listen and not even have to rewind anything. Cassette players you used to have to rewind and wait. Sometimes you'd try to rewind it just right to a certain part of the song you wanted to hear. People don't even listen to the whole song anymore.

Voting—People can't even get their sorry asses to the voting booth because they have no clue how important it is to their livelihood.

There are so many other things I could go on about in regards to the laziness of people throughout the world. It's no super secret. What people don't realize is that this laziness is having an effect on the whole country. People are now sheeple and could care less about the fact they're about to lose their country.

If you follow along closely to the next few chapters, you may be surprised by how things are not always as they seem and what is about to really happen in this world of ours. So, keep your reading glasses on because I want you to see what I'm saying and not let the ol' "lazy" eyes wander away when there is some great stuff to come.

Book 'em, Dano!
Stupid Is as Stupid
Does!

After looking at all the politicians that don't deserve to be in their position, I had to look at where they come from. It appears that there is an ancestral lineage to stupidity and I figure that the stories below, which I found through various sites on the Internet, must have been quite a shock to other family members. I figured that if President Carter could have a brother who sold Billy Beer and did some other knuckleheaded things, then some of these idiots you're about to read about could possibly be related to others in the political arena. I know it's a stretch, but I wouldn't bet against the possibility.

So, let's take a look at stupid is as stupid does.

A woman gets arrested at her step-son's Boy Scout meeting. An officer proceeds to do a demonstration of his drug-sniffing dog and is led to the woman's purse where the dog sniffed out a bag of marijuana.

A guy walks into a convenient store with a shotgun and demands all the money from the register. The clerk does as he is told and puts all the money in a bag. Then the robber sees a bottle of liquor on the shelf behind the counter. The robber tells the clerk to add it to the bag, but the clerk refuses with an explanation, "I don't believe you're twenty-one or over." Telling the clerk that he was definitely older than twenty-one the clerk still refuses to believe it. To prove the clerk wrong the robber takes out his license and shows it to the clerk. Problem solved and the clerk agrees by putting the liquor in the bag. The robber then leaves the store as the clerk calls police to inform them of the robbery and the address of his driver's license. The robber is arrested two hours later.

A woman parks her car and while away, it is stolen. When filling out the report, the woman mentions to the officer that her cell phone was in the car. The officer thinking quickly, calls her cell phone and the thief answers. Telling the thief that he saw the for-sale ad and is interest in buying it, they arrange for a time to meet. The thief shows up and is arrested.

A man decides he is going to rob a Bank of America. Not very literate, he waits in line to hand the teller a note that reads, "this iz a stickup. Put all your muny in this bag." While waiting he begins to wonder if anyone saw him while writing his note and they might call the police. He ends up leaving the bank and crosses the street to visit a Wells Fargo Bank. After waiting a few minutes he hands his note to the teller who reads it realizes through the spelling errors that the man is an idiot and informs the man that the message is written on a Bank of America slip and can't be authorized with this bank. Looking somewhat defeated, the man says, "okay," and leaves. The teller then calls the police who go arrest the man who is waiting in line back at the B of A.

A drug defendant said that he'd been searched without a warrant. The prosecutor said that the police didn't need a warrant because the bulge in the man's jacket could have been a gun. "Nonsense," says the defendant. He hands over the jacket so the judge can take a closer look at it. The judge begins laughing hysterically, after discovering a packet of cocaine in the pocket, and it takes five minutes to recompose himself.

A man was on trial for holding up a convenience store. While in the district court the man fired his attorney. The Assistant DA said the man was doing a fair job of defending himself until the store's manager testified that the man was indeed the robber. The man jumped up and yelled, "I should have blown your (expletive) head off." Pausing a moment, he then quickly added, "If I'd been the one there." Twenty minutes later the jury convicted the man and recommended a thirty-year sentence.

A twenty-one-year-old kid walks up to two patrol officers who are showing off the computer equipment in their car that locates felons. When he asks how the system works, the officer asks the young man for his ID. Entering the information into the computer, moments later the young man is arrested for a two-year-old crime committed in another state.

In a small town, a student decides to rob a convenient store. Not realizing he is wearing his letterman's jacket with his name, Dana, on it. He is the only male Dana in the whole town.

In the dead of winter, a high school student decides it would be a good idea to rob the local mini-mart. He walks to the store with a gun and steals $50. The police are only minutes away and able to track the young man's footprints directly to his front door.

After robbing a convenient store, two teenage boys are chased by a group of cops. Desperately trying to escape, they climb over a high chain-link fence. The cops stop chasing when they realize that the boys climbed into the local prison. They called the security in the compound to find the boys.

A man walks into a convenience store and asks for all the money in the register. The take being too small, the robber ties up the clerk and proceeds to work the counter for three hours until the police show up and grab him.

A man strolls into a drug store, pulls a gun, and tells everyone he's robbing the place. Pulling a Hefty bag face mask over his head he realizes that he can't see because he'd forgotten to put eye holes in.

Now, I don't know if all of these are true or just someone's wild imagination, but after judging the politics of this world and realizing that our education system is not the best, and TV shows like Jerry Springer get top ratings…well, perhaps these things did happen.

A Perfect World

I t's not so ass-backwards to want a world I remember while growing up. Though it wasn't perfect then and it sure as hell isn't perfect now, the difference has been an in-your-face, up-close-and-personal change. I gave my rant about topics that I care dearly for. I gave my opinion as to the problems in our country and though I tried to joke about much of it, keeping it somewhat light-hearted, the truth of the matter is that this country is in a sad place right now.

Our tax system is way out of hand and eventually will have to change. There is no way you can go to the well forever and expect that it will always be full. The politicians in this country seem to think that pockets are much deeper than they are in reality, perhaps that is the reason so many states are failing or in such serious debt that they too will need a bailout from the Fed.

There are reasons yet to be produced in proper form as to the reason our country gets deeper and deeper into financial trouble. It's not for the lack of want. People in the US want their toys and unfortunately are willing to borrow to get them. Of course this is also good for the country because if everyone had to wait until they had enough money, items would sit on the showroom floor collecting dust.

The devil is in the debt, but it's the people who are selling their souls and accumulating that debt which in turn keeps the devil in a very busy and happy state of existence. A friend mentioned something to me and though I haven't truly taken the time to consider the ramifications of it, if there really are any to begin with, he commented, "Instead of bailing them out, why didn't the government let those businesses fail and just give everyone in America $1,000,000. The majority of Americans won't save their money, so we may have spent our way out. The IRS could have taxed them and people still would have spent on new cars, paying off debt, buying houses, paying for education.

Can't we just all agree to win again? Let's tell our young kids that winning is okay and that by not caring, thinking it's okay to lose, we've come close to be completely socialized and ruining our great country permanently. Let's teach our youth that we once had an identity to be proud of. We once knew who we were and what we stood for. While we're at it, let's teach them that they have it easy as kids and life can be just as great as an adult, all it takes is a little bit of continuous effort on their part. Parents, can you join me here and let your kids know what life was like and how we didn't sit around waiting for our parents to give us anything. Our parents will never have to apologize for stealing our abilities away. They taught us that if we wanted something, we had to work for it. Today's kids aren't being taught that vital component of survival and unfortunately, it has weaken our society.

To the generation from the sixties, seventies, and eighties, I'd like you to join me in a massive game that spreads across the country. On your next available weekend go into the local mall, walk into the closest electronics store, one that sells CDs, and look for the youngest sales person you can find. Ask that person where they keep the latest vinyl or eight-track. Tell them you'd like to get the latest Boston, Chicago, or Asia album. They'll probably direct you to MapQuest or give you a Garmin device. Then, pretend to forget the name of an album and ask if they can direct you to the closest pay phone so you can make a long distant call to your cousins, Jackson Brown and Bryan Adams. When they don't know what you're talking about or ask you if you have a cell phone, give them the deer-in-the-headlight look and simply say, "If you just direct me to the vinyl aisle I'll find it myself." Then add, "What's a cell phone?"

One of the great pleasures from my past is recalling how I would play the latest album over and over and as loud as I possibly could. Yes, I too was a teenage kid and I understand the need for great music that blares out of the speakers so loud that you can barely hear mom or dad yelling, "Turn that damn thing off!" Now, those damn things are so abundant in scope to my past. We as a society really have given up on our youth when we allow texting, TV, or anything other than family conversation at the dinner table. Do people still gather together for dinner these days? I should hope so. If not, then again, kids will never get to know the greatness of being part of a family. I've heard it from so many people all across the country, "Dinners at the table with my family were some of the best times I had while growing up." There's a reason for this and none of it is about being self-centered.

There is a lot to do in the beautiful country of ours. Hell, there's a lot to do in the world, but at this moment my focus is on the home front. I know there are lawsuits and people are pissed off for one reason or another, but really, it can't be handled by either side admitting they too are at fault, at least partially? Though I call attorneys vampires, I know that there are a lot of well-meaning men and women in this occupation that fight for the rights of people everywhere and these people are needed. If you're an ambulance chaser, and you know if you are, then I could only wish that you'd slowly wean yourself away from dirty money and step up to a level of integrity that you thought you possessed when you first decided to get a degree in law.

It seems I ranted about a lot of issues regarding parenting and how it's had an awful effect on society as a whole. There are many working men and women who are pulling more weight regarding the family life than their stay-at-home spouses. If things aren't going the way you think they should, if you ever catch yourself ranting and raving about your kids or your spouse, well, most likely it's you with the problem.

In cleaning up and creating my perfect world the biggest things I wish I could have an effect on would be the government, the politicians, and the taxes. I guess there is some truth to the idea of being "above the law" when our politicians don't have to pay the same taxes or follow the same rules as the people they're supposed to represent. I think the politicians have misconstrued their role and mistaken the word "lead" for "represent." They're supposed to represent the people of the cities, counties, and states, yet they take an active role in leading themselves to products that the average citizen just doesn't or isn't allowed to receive. What a scam! What I really can't believe is having a country that is so divided that the leaders of our "free" world would start a lawsuit against one of its own. Really, illegal immigration is as it implies...illegal, yet the president sides with those who are here illegally. Neither you or I could go to any other country and work or use their amenities and not have to pay for it. That's as close to your mom looking you in the face and telling you she loves everyone else's kids more than you. There is absolutely no loyalty from this president to the country. I guess when he promised change we should have asked for far more specifics than he allotted.

Again, I don't expect a perfect world, but one that worked congruently toward a greater objective and allowed people to finally get back to winning would be nice. If we continue to promote the ignorance of the nation by having television shows that show how stupid people can be, then we're done for. I don't necessarily believe we should be monitored 24/7, but setting a precedence is vital if we are to regain our strength and become a nation that truly leads again.

I guess the overall trick to regaining our country's ability to lead again is to cut through the crap and push politicians out of office that take from lobbyists or have accepted the lie that no one wins. "Give me liberty or give me death," is a far cry from "Give me an iPod, iPad, Nintendo 64, Grand Theft Auto, a new 4G cell phone..."

Somebody, please—give me a break, and then send me a F'n thank you card!

The End

Made in the USA
Charleston, SC
04 September 2011